BAZI STRUCTURES
&
Structural Useful Gods

METAL 金

庚 Geng
辛 Xin

格局與格局用神

BaZi Structures & Structural Useful Gods
Metal Structure

The author can be reached at:

Mastery Academy of Chinese Metaphysics Sdn. Bhd. (611143-A)
19-3, The Boulevard, Mid Valley City,
59200 Kuala Lumpur, Malaysia.
Tel   : +603-2284 8080
Fax   : +603-2284 1218
Email   : info@masteryacademy.com
Website: www.masteryacademy.com

DISCLAIMER:

The author, Joey Yap and the publisher, JY Books Sdn Bhd, have made their best efforts to produce this high quality, informative and helpful book. They have verified the technical accuracy of the information and contents of this book. Any information pertaining to the events, occurrences, dates and other details relating to the person or persons, dead or alive, and to the companies have been verified to the best of their abilities based on information obtained or extracted from various websites, newspaper clippings and other public media. However, they make no representation or warranties of any kind with regard to the contents of this book and accept no liability of any kind for any losses or damages caused or alleged to be caused directly or indirectly from using the information contained herein.

Published by JY Books Sdn. Bhd. (659134-T)

Table of Contents

Table of Contents

About The Chinese Metaphysics Reference Series

Reference Series

The Chinese Metaphysics Reference Series of books are designed primarily to be used as complimentary textbooks for scholars, students, researchers, teachers and practitioners of Chinese Metaphysics.

The goal is to provide quick easy reference tables, diagrams and charts, facilitating the study and practice of various Chinese Metaphysics subjects including Feng Shui, BaZi, Yi Jing, Zi Wei, Liu Ren, Ze Ri, Ta Yi, Qi Men and Mian Xiang.

This series of books are intended as reference text and educational materials principally for the academic syllabuses of the **Mastery Academy of Chinese Metaphysics**. The contents have also been formatted so that Feng Shui Masters and other teachers of Chinese Metaphysics will always have a definitive source of reference at hand, when teaching or applying their art.

Because each school of Chinese Metaphysics is different, the Reference Series of books usually do not contain any specific commentaries, application methods or explanations on the theory behind the formulas presented in its contents. This is to ensure that the contents can be used freely and independently by all Feng Shui Masters and teachers of Chinese Metaphysics without conflict.

If you would like to study or learn the applications of any of the formulas presented in the Reference Series of books, we recommend that you undertake the courses offered by Joey Yap and his team of Instructors at the Mastery Academy of Chinese Metaphysics.

Titles offers in the Reference Series:

1. The Chinese Metaphysics Compendium
2. Dong Gong Date Selection
3. Earth Study Discern Truth
4. Xuan Kong Da Gua Structure Reference Book
5. San Yuan Dragon Gate Eight Formations Water Method
6. Xuan Kong Da Gua Ten Thousand Year Calendar
7. Plum Blossom Divination Reference Book
8. The Date Selection Compendium (Book 1) - The 60 Jia Zi Attributes
9. BaZi Structures & Structural Useful Gods Reference Series

Preface

The study and practice of BaZi is an infinitely rewarding and intriguing one, with literally an inexhaustible depth and range from which we can mine our information on a person's character, temperament, life outlook and personal destiny. The simplest data – your birth date and time – can yield a rich treasure trove of knowledge, most of which can help shed new light on old perceptions.

The idea for this BaZi Structures and Structural Useful God Reference Series came out of a common need among my BaZi students, many of whom wanted to learn more about how the various structures in BaZi are derived. This series was therefore created to help students learn and absorb the methods and techniques in which a structure is created and developed mainly from a classical standpoint.

While initially it was my idea to create one BaZi Structures book to accommodate all 10 Heavenly Stems (Day Masters), I soon found out that it would not be a book that could reasonably be used by anyone – because it would be too heavy to lift! So I decided to break it apart into five different books, with each one corresponding to each Element. The book you're holding in your hands is on Metal Structures, for both Geng 庚 and Xin 辛 Water Day Masters.

There are many traditional sources available on the BaZi structures, and the derivation of those structures. One of the more well-known texts is the *Qiong Tong Bao Jian* 窮通寶鑑, written by a famous master, *Xu Le Wu* 徐樂吾. Another popular BaZi scholar of recent past who contributed a lot to mainstream BaZi theories, especially those relating to structures, is *Wei Qian Li* 韋千里.

It's difficult for most students to have access to this information because it's scattered about in various texts and documents, and also – all of it is available only in Chinese. It was my intention, therefore, to compile this information into one convenient source, and to present the transliterated version of these traditional texts for the modern, English-speaking practitioner and student without losing the essence of the original.

To derive a structure and structural Useful God in BaZi, one must know and understand the Day Master and the month of birth, and its variations in a BaZi chart. There are traditional methods on how this is derived, and there are newer interpretations on these methods.

As such, different practitioners and teachers have different methods and formats to derive these structures, and it is recommended that you use the techniques outlined in this book with care and thought. As always, there is much merit in using traditional practices, but students who are learning BaZi should use this under the supervision of a teacher in order to better understand the subject. A good teacher will help you understand the different ways of interpreting these traditional texts.

Do note that these texts should not be taken literally. Different masters may agree or disagree with the classical commentaries included here, and as a student, it's important for you to know the reasons why. Better yet, it's important for you to know those reasons and then go on to form your own conclusions, based on your understanding of the various interpretations.

For that reason, this book was designed to be a reference accompaniment for the students of my BaZi Mastery Series, where you'll be able to get the guidance you need in interpreting these traditional methods. I encourage you to take a class because it will help to place this material in context and give you the added knowledge you need to help you make the most of the information contained within this book. Each and every structure in this book could be its own chapter, because it can literally explain a person and his or her modus operandi!

I hope you enjoy your research on this subject, and here's to many pleasurable hours of BaZi Structural study!

Warm regards,

Joey Yap
June 2009

Author's personal websites :
www.joeyyap.com | www.fengshuilogy.com (Personal blog)

Academy websites :
www.masteryacademy.com | www.masteryjournal.com | www.maelearning.com

Follow Joey's current updates on Twitter :
www.twitter.com/joeyyap

MASTERY ACADEMY
OF CHINESE METAPHYSICS™

At **www.masteryacademy.com**, you will find some useful tools to ascertain key information about the Feng Shui of a property or for the study of Astrology.

The Joey Yap Flying Stars Calculator can be utilised to plot your home or office Flying Stars chart. To find out your personal best directions, use the 8 Mansions Calculator. To learn more about your personal Destiny, you can use the Joey Yap BaZi Ming Pan Calculator to plot your Four Pillars of Destiny – you just need to have your date of birth (day, month, year) and time of birth.

For more information about BaZi, Xuan Kong or Flying Star Feng Shui, or if you wish to learn more about these subjects with Joey Yap, logon to the Mastery Academy of Chinese Metaphysics website at **www.masteryacademy.com.**

MASTERY ACADEMY
E-LEARNING CENTER
www.maelearning.com

www.maelearning.com

Bookmark this address on your computer, and visit this newly-launched website today. With the E-Learning Center, knowledge of Chinese Metaphysics is a mere 'click' away!

Our E-Learning Center consists of 3 distinct components.

1. Online Courses
These shall comprise of 3 Programs: our Online Feng Shui Program, Online BaZi Program, and Online Mian Xiang Program. Each lesson contains a video lecture, slide presentation and downloadable course notes.

2. MA Live!
With MA Live!, Joey Yap's workshops, tutorials, courses and seminars on various Chinese Metaphysics subjects broadcasted right to your computer screen. Better still, participants will not only get to see and hear Joey talk 'live', but also get to engage themselves directly in the event and more importantly, TALK to Joey via the MA Live! interface. All the benefits of a live class, minus the hassle of actually having to attend one!

3. Video-On-Demand (VOD)
Get immediate streaming-downloads of the Mastery Academy's wide range of educational DVDs, right on your computer screen. No more shipping costs and waiting time to be incurred!

Study at your own pace, and interact with your Instructor and fellow students worldwide… at your own convenience and privacy. With our E-Learning Center, knowledge of Chinese Metaphysics is brought DIRECTLY to you in all its clarity, with illustrated presentations and comprehensive notes expediting your learning curve!

Welcome to the Mastery Academy's E-LEARNING CENTER…YOUR virtual gateway to Chinese Metaphysics mastery!

Introduction - Metal Day Masters

Tough, just, righteous, fair and square just about describe Metal Day Masters best. Of course, if we are able to identify the inherent or ingrained characteristics of Geng 庚 Day Masters and Xin 辛 Day Masters, all the better.

Geng Metal people are tough, able to withstand adversity and hardship, and will usually prefer to take matters into their own hands and do things themselves – to ensure that the results are to their liking. Depending on the strength of their BaZi Chart as well as a myriad of other factors, Geng Metal Day Masters do have their own share of weaknesses as well.

Indeed, Geng Metal Day Masters tend to be inflexible, hasty and stubborn, by nature. It is, however, their pride and ego that may lead to their downfall, more so if they persist in pursuing matters in an aggressive, foolhardy manner. Nevertheless, they are also altruistic and magnanimous, and value their relationship with loved ones highly. And as one may easily guess, Geng Metal Day Masters do have strong characters.

Xin Metal people are natural attention-grabbers; something ingrained within their very nature, that they may not even be consciously aware of it. They like being in the limelight, and being the showcase of the event.

While Xin Metal Day Masters may appear to be tough and even obstinate at times, the subtle, gentle approach works best in getting them to listen to you, or your advice. And just like their Geng Metal counterparts, they can be sentimental and loving - or stubborn, proud and difficult to deal with, depending on how one approaches them.

Geng (庚) Metal Day Master

Overview:

Geng 庚 Metal is Yang Metal. It represents tough, durable Metal such as steel, tin and iron. Unsurprisingly, Geng Metal usually assumes a rugged, even rough appearance.

Nevertheless, Ding Fire is still needed to 'polish' and enable Geng Metal to shine and be appreciated for what it really is. Since Wood produces Fire, the presence of both Wood and Fire in the BaZi Chart of Geng Metal Day Masters would allow them to become skillful, intelligent and even famous in life. Indeed, the presence of these Useful Gods shall allow Geng Metal Day Masters to prosper.

Since real-life examples of Geng Metal include the sword and axe, Geng Metal Day Masters usually possess an endurance and stamina beyond those of other Day Masters. Being tough, resilient and hands-on, Geng Metal Day Masters will not hesitate to do something themselves, if they think their approach is the better one in getting something done.

Despite their strong leadership skills and generally strong personalities, however, Geng Metal Day Masters are altruistic types, who value friendship and brotherhood. Unsurprisingly, they can also be sentimental – just like their Xin Metal counterparts – when it comes to placing a premium on their 'special' or personal relationships.

Geng 庚 Metal Day Master, Born in First Month 正月

Yin 寅 (Tiger) Month
February 4th – March 5th

Do note that the dates provided above are subject to slight yearly variations. Please refer to your Annual Tong Shu or Joey Yap's Ten Thousand Year Calendar for the accurate dates for each year.

| **Day Master** Geng 庚 Metal | **Month** Yin 寅 (Tiger) |

日元 **Day Master**	月 **Month**
庚 *Geng* **Yang Metal**	寅 *Yin* **Tiger** **Yang Wood**

For a Geng Metal Day Master born in a Yin (Tiger) Month, an Indirect Wealth Structure is formed where Jia Wood is revealed as one of the Heavenly Stems.

Where Bing Fire is revealed as one of the Heavenly Stems, a Seven Killings Structure is formed.

Where Wu Earth is revealed as one of the Heavenly Stems, an Indirect Resource Structure is formed.

Should, however, neither Jia Wood nor Bing Fire nor Wu Earth happen to be revealed within the Heavenly Stems, one should select the BaZi Chart's most prominent Qi attribute at one's discretion.

| Day Master | Geng 庚 Metal | Month | Yin 寅 (Tiger) |

庚金水喜用神提要 Regulating Useful God Reference Guide

正月 First Month

Tiger

月 Month	用神 Useful God				
1st Month 正月 **Yin 寅 (Tiger) Month**	戊 *Wu* **Yang** **Earth**	甲 *Jia* **Yang** **Wood**	壬 *Ren* **Yang** **Water**	丙 *Bing* **Yang** **Fire**	丁 *Ding* **Yin** **Fire**

For a Yin (Tiger) Month, Wu Earth, Jia Wood, Ren Water, Bing Fire and Ding Fire are its Regulating Useful Gods.

Bing Fire should be employed as a Useful God to `warm' this Geng Metal Day Master.

Since Earth is still `leaden' and `thick' in a Yin (Tiger) Month, it would invariably `bury' or `conceal' Metal. As such, Jia Wood is needed to `loosen' and hence weaken Earth.

Where Fire is present in abundance, however, Earth may be used to weaken and keep Fire under control. Where the relevant Earthly Branches form a Fire Structure, Ren Water may be used to keep excess Fire Qi under control.

| Day Master | Geng 庚 Metal | Month | Yin 寅 (Tiger) |

4th day of February – 5th day of March, Gregorian Calendar

Tiger

Where Jia Wood, Wu Earth and Bing Fire are all present in the BaZi Chart of a Geng Metal Day Master born in a Yin (Tiger) Month, the Qi of Wood and Fire (Wealth and Officer Stars) - would exceed those of Earth and Metal. It is desirable for all three stems to reveal in the Heavenly Stems. This is a special chart.

Wood is strong and thriving in the spring month, while Metal is weak. As such, Earth should be used to produce and further strengthen Metal, which would then be able to use Jia Wood as a good Wealth Star.

It would, however, be unfavorable for this Geng Metal Day Master to encounter Water. This is because Water weakens Metal, and also produces Wood.

A Geng Metal Day Master born in an hour where Fire and Earth are strong may easily form a Yin (Tiger) and Wu (Horse) Fire formation. Under such circumstances, Metal and Water may be employed as Useful Gods, in bringing balance to this Geng Metal Day Master.

正
月

First Month

Tiger

Day Master Geng 庚 Metal		**Month** Yin 寅 (Tiger)

Additional Attributes

格局 **Structural Star**	偏財 Indirect Wealth	七殺 Seven Killings
用神 **Useful God**	Jia 甲 Wood	Bing 丙 Fire
Conditions	Bing Fire and Jia Wood should, preferably, be present in the Month Pillar Earthly Branches, as well as revealed within the same palace. Where such a scenario is possible, this Geng Metal Day Master shall certainly succeed in life.	
Positive Circumstances	Bing Fire and Jia Wood penetrating to the Heavenly Stems at the same time	
Negative Circumstances	Clash of the Monthly Branch	

格局 **Structural Star**	正官 Direct Officer
用神 **Useful God**	Ding 丁 Fire
Conditions	Where Ji Earth (Resource Star) is present but Gui Water (Hurting Officer Star) is absent, this Geng Metal Day Master could still prosper in life.
Positive Circumstances	Only Ji Earth may be suitably employed as a Useful God. Wu Earth, as the Resource Star, would not be able to substitute Ji Earth.
Negative Circumstances	Gui Water, as a Hurting Officer Star, is seen penetrating through the Heavenly Stems.

Day Master Geng 庚 Metal	**Month** Yin 寅 (Tiger)
Additional Attributes	

格局 **Structural Star**	七殺 Seven Killings
用神 **Useful God**	Bing 丙 Fire
Conditions	Where the Earthly Branches form a Fire Formation (which is a Seven Killings) along with a Ren Water also revealing in the Heavenly Stems, this Geng Metal Day Master shall enjoy favourable outcomes in life.
Positive Circumstances	Presence of Ren Water penetrated to the Heavenly Stems of the chart.
Negative Circumstances	Where Ren Water and Gui Water do not penetrate through the Heavenly Stems, this Geng Metal Day Master may be afflicted by physical disability or illness in life.

* *Bing Fire and Jia Wood are the most-preferred Useful Gods.*

***Where Fire is missing from this Geng Metal Day Master's BaZi Chart, he or she may be afflicted by poverty in life.*

正月
First Month

Tiger

| Day Master | Geng 庚 Metal | | Month | Yin 寅 (Tiger) |

Summary

- A Geng Metal Day Master born in a Yin (Tiger) Month should not use Wu Earth, (Indirect Resource). Yang Earth is unable to support Geng Metal.

- It is unfavorable for a Geng Metal Direct Officer Structure to see a Hurting Officer Star revealed in the Heavenly Stems of the chart.

- Where Earth is present in abundance in the Chart having Jia Wood revealed in the Heavenly Stems is highly desirable. When this criteria is met, this Geng Metal Day Master shall enjoy a fulfilling life.

- A Geng Metal Day Master would, however, not benefit at all, should Yi Wood happen to be revealed instead of Jia Wood. Yi Wood is insufficient in controlling the abundant Earth.

Geng 庚 Metal Day Master, Born in Second Month 二月

Mao 卯 (Rabbit) Month
March 6th – April 4th

Do note that the dates provided above are subject to slight yearly variations. Please refer to your Annual Tong Shu or Joey Yap's Ten Thousand Year Calendar for the accurate dates for each year.

Day Master Geng 庚 Metal | **Month** Mao 卯 (Rabbit)

Rabbit

日元 **Day Master**	月 **Month**
庚 *Geng* **Yang Metal**	卯 *Mao* **Rabbit** **Yin Wood**

For a Xin Metal Day Master born in a Mao (Rabbit) Month, a Direct Wealth Structure is formed where Yi Wood is revealed (or not revealed) as one of the Heavenly Stems in the chart.

| Day Master | Geng 庚 Metal | | Month | Mao 卯 (Rabbit) |

喜用神提要 **Regulating Useful God Reference Guide**

月 **Month**	用神 **Useful God**
2nd Month 二月 Mao 卯 (Rabbit) Month	丁 甲 庚 丙 *Ding* *Jia* *Geng* *Bing* **Yin Fire** **Yang Wood** **Yang Metal** **Yang Fire**

卯 Rabbit

For a Mao (Rabbit) Month, Ding Fire, Jia Wood, Geng Metal and Bing Fire are its Regulating Useful Gods.

In a Mao (Rabbit) Month, Geng Metal is `dark' but strong in nature. As such, more attention should be paid in using Ding Fire to `illuminate' this Geng Metal Day Master. Meanwhile, Jia Wood may be `borrowed' and used to lure out Ding Fire.

The preceding scenario comes full-circle, with Geng Metal being used to `cut' and hence keep Jia Wood under control.

In the absence of Ding Fire, Bing Fire may be used as a substitute.

Day Master Geng 庚 Metal   Month   Mao 卯 (Rabbit)

6th day of March – 4th day of April, Gregorian Calendar

In the Mao (Rabbit) Month, Wood Qi is at its peak or most prosperous in spring.

As such, while Wood keeps Metal under control, Ji Earth – as a Resource Star - may be used to produce and further strengthen Metal.

Of the Five Elements, Wood would be the strongest in spring; perhaps even overly strong at this time of the year. It would hence there is a tendency for this Geng Metal Day Master to form Direct Wealth Structures, which would also weaken Geng Metal in the process.

Consequently, only Earth may be suitably used to produce and hence strengthen this Geng Metal Day Master.

The hour of birth is taken into consideration. Where Wood and Fire happen to be strong in the hour of birth, it would be preferable for this Day Master not to encounter Water. This is because Water will produce and further strengthen Wood.

A Geng Metal Day Master born in a Mao (Rabbit) Month entering Earth or Metal Luck, who forms or combines with a Metal frame is desirable. The person would find his or her enjoying excellent fortunes during this period of time.

| Day Master | Geng 庚 Metal | Month | Mao 卯 (Rabbit) |

Commentary

In addition to the preceding narratives on the potential Structures and scenarios resulting from a Geng Metal Day Master born in a Mao (Rabbit) Month, the following circumstances also play their respective roles in determining the overall strength of this Day Master's BaZi Chart.

Note:

- A Geng Metal Day Master born in a Mao (Rabbit) Month should employ Ding Fire and Jia Wood as its Useful Gods.

- Where Jia Wood is found in the Earthly Branches and Heavenly Stems of this Geng Metal Day Master's BaZi Chart – but Companion (Metal) and Resource (Earth) Stars are absent – the resultant Follow the Wealth Structure formed would allow this Geng Metal Day Master to prosper in life. This is a special structure.

- Ding Fire is the preferred Useful God for Geng Metal Day Master born in a Mao (Rabbit) Month. Ren Water should be prevented from penetrating through the Heavenly Stems, since it will combine Ding Fire away.

- Yi Wood should also be prevented from penetrating through the Heavenly Stems, since it will combine with this Geng Metal Day Master to produce, unfortunately, `worthless' Metal.

- Where Bing Fire or Ding Fire does not penetrate through the Heavenly Stems of the chart, this Geng Metal Day Master may not really be able to upkeep his or her standard of living; even though he or she insists on maintaining a certain standard of living.

- In addition, Geng Metal in a Yin (Tiger) or Mao (Rabbit) Month, the Qi of Geng Metal is fast-dwindling or receding. Ironically, it may not really be favorable to this Geng Metal Day Master, should Earth – as a Resource Star – happen to be found in abundance, since there is also the risk of abundant Earth `burying' and hence `suffocating' Geng Metal.

Rabbit

Rabbit

Day Master Geng 庚 **Metal**　　**Month** Mao 卯 **(Rabbit)**

Additional Attributes

格局 **Structural Star**	正官 Direct Officer	偏財 Indirect Wealth
用神 **Useful God**	Ding 丁 Fire	Jia 甲 Wood
Conditions	This Geng Metal Day Master should, preferably, be rooted in Earthly Branches, in order for him or her to succeed in life.	
Positive Circumstances	This Geng Metal Day Master should be rooted in the Earthly Branches. This denotes that the Geng Metal is stable. Being rooted, this Geng is able to benefit from the Ding Fire and Jia Wood energy.	
Negative Circumstances	If this Geng Metal Day Master is not rooted in the Earthly Branches, he or she may suffer from poor health in life.	

Day Master	Geng 庚 Metal	Month	Mao 卯 (Rabbit)

Additional Attributes

格局 Structural Star	偏財 Indirect Wealth
用神 Useful God	Jia 甲 Wood
Conditions	Where the Earthly Branches are mainly Wood - which forms a strong Wealth Structure - the absence of Companion (Metal) and Resource (Earth) Stars will result in a *Follow the Wealth* Structure being formed. When the formation is successful, this person shall prosper and become immensely wealthy in life.
Positive Circumstances	Where Jia Wood (Indirect Wealth Star) – is revealed, in the Heavenly Stems.
Negative Circumstances	The Heavenly Stems encounter Friend or Companion Stars. Where Jia Wood (Indirect Wealth Star) and Yi Wood (Direct Wealth appears at the same time - the role of Jia Wood would be useless.

* This Geng Metal Day Master should be rooted in the Earthly Branches.

** Ding Fire and Jia Wood are the preferred Useful Gods for this Geng Metal Day Master.

二月 Second Month

Rabbit

17

| **Day Master** Geng 庚 Metal | **Month** Mao 卯 (Rabbit) |

Summary

- Geng Metal should be rooted in the Earthly Branches of the BaZi Chart. The best-case scenario would be to have a Shen (Monkey) Earthly Branch present in the BaZi Chart.

- As far as Wealth Stars are concerned, Jia Wood – the Indirect Wealth Star is prefeered over Yi Wood – the Direct Wealth Star. Where Yi Wood is present, it should not be allowed to combine with this Geng Metal Day Master. Combining would render the Wealth element useless. In the life of a man, he would totally loose his character, turn against friends in favor of a woman. Or worst, loose his wealth as a result.

- It would be best to avoid having Wu Earth the Indirect Resource Star or Ji Earth the Direct Resource Star - penetrate through the Heavenly Stems.

- Where the Ding Fire (Direct Officer Star) is chosen as the Useful God, Gui Water (Hurting Officer Star) should be prevented from penetrating through the Heavenly Stems.

Rabbit

二月 Second Month

Geng 庚 Metal Day Master, Born in Third Month 三月

Chen 辰 (Dragon) Month
April 5th - May 5th

Do note that the dates provided above are subject to slight yearly variations. Please refer to your Annual Tong Shu or Joey Yap's Ten Thousand Year Calendar for the accurate dates for each year.

Day Master Geng 庚 Metal   **Month** Chen 辰 (Dragon)

三月 Third Month

Dragon

日元 **Day Master**	月 **Month**
庚 Geng Yang Metal	辰 Chen Dragon Yang Earth

For a Geng Metal Day Master born in a Chen (Dragon) Month, an Indirect Resource Structure is formed where Wu Earth is revealed as one of the Heavenly Stems.

Where Yi Wood is revealed as one of the Heavenly Stems, a Direct Wealth Structure is formed.

Where Gui Water is revealed as one of the Heavenly Stems, a Hurting Officer Structure is formed.

Should, however, neither Yi Wood nor Wu Earth nor Gui Water happen to be revealed within the Heavenly Stems, one should select a Structure according to the BaZi Chart's most prominent Qi attribute at one's discretion.

| Day Master | Geng 庚 Metal | | Month | Chen 辰 (Dragon) |

庚金水喜用神提要 **Regulating Useful God Reference Guide**

月 **Month**	用神 **Useful God**
3rd Month 三月 **Chen** 辰 **(Dragon) Month**	甲 *Jia* **Yang Wood** 丁 *Ding* **Yin Fire** 壬 *Ren* **Yang Water** 癸 *Gui* **Yin Water**

Dragon

For a Chen (Dragon) Month, Jia Wood, Ding Fire, Ren Water and Gui Water are its most important Regulating Useful Gods.

Ding Fire may be suitably used as a Useful God for Geng Metal, since the latter is Yang Metal and hence `tough' Metal. And Ding Fire forges this metal to make it 'useful'.

Where Earth is strong, Jia Wood may be used to keep it under control. Geng Metal, however, should not be used to `cut' and weaken Wood.

Where the Earthly Branches contain an excess of Fire Qi, Gui Water may be used to keep Fire under control. Likewise, where the Heavenly Stems contain an excess of Fire Qi, Ren Water may be used to keep Fire under control.

| Day Master Geng 庚 Metal | Month Chen 辰 (Dragon) |

5th day of April – 5th day of May, Gregorian Calendar

The Chen (Dragon) Earthly Branch – contains the Hidden Stems of Wu Earth, Yi Wood and Gui Water. The Earth Qi features prominently in a Chen (Dragon) Month when the Wu Earth appears in the Heavenly Stems.

As such, where Earth produces Geng Metal, while Water simultaneously produces Wood, this Geng Metal Day Master would prosper and become wealthy in life. It is necessary for the Wood to control and loosen the Earth for Metal Qi to prosper.

Where Metal is exceptionally strong, Fire may be used to counter and hence keep Metal Qi under control. Where there is sufficient Wood Qi to produce Fire Qi, this Geng Metal Day Master's Wealth and Officer Stars shall thrive, therefore allowing this Day Master to become powerful and authoritative in life.

Dragon

| Day Master | Geng 庚 Metal | Month | Chen 辰 (Dragon) |

Commentary

In addition to the preceding narratives on the potential Structures and scenarios resulting from a Geng Metal Day Master born in a Chen (Dragon) Month, the following circumstances also play their respective roles in determining the overall strength of this Day Master's BaZi Chart.

辰
Dragon

Note:

- Ding Fire and Jia Wood are the preferred Useful Gods for this Geng Metal Day Master.

- Ren Water and Gui Water should be avoided, if possible, since both are 'diseased' (as they are stored in the Chen for too long) and would hence weaken this Geng Metal Day Master considerably.

- Jia Wood, if present, is suitably countered by Geng Metal; Bing Fire should preferably be countered by Ren Water; Wu Earth should preferably be countered Jia Wood; Ren Water should preferably be countered by Wu Earth; while Geng Metal should preferably be countered by Ding Fire. Where this cycle of Five Elements exist in this chart, a life of greatness is expected.

- Where Ding Fire and Jia Wood are both revealed – but Friend and Rob Wealth Stars (meaning Metal Elements) are not seen penetrating through the Heavenly Stems – this Geng Metal Day Master shall enjoy success in his or her career.

- Where the Earthly Branches form a 'Four Dragons' Earth Formation, Jia Wood is needed to penetrate through the Heavenly Stems. Otherwise, this Geng Metal Day Master may suffer from loneliness and poverty in life.

- Where Yi Wood is used to replace Jia Wood, the former's strength is only limited to 'loosening' the Earth element. Under such circumstances, this Geng Metal Day Master may lack the drive and independence required to succeed in his or her career.

- Where Ding Fire is revealed in the Heavenly Stems– but Jia Wood remains hidden inside the Earthly Branches– this Geng Metal Day Master shall belong to a learned, knowledgeable person.

- Where Jia Wood is revealed in the Heavenly Stems– but Ding Fire is hidden in the Earthly Branches– this Geng Metal Day Master may, however, enjoy unexpected success in life.

- Where Ding Fire and Jia Wood both remain hidden inside the Earthly Branches, this Geng Metal Day Master shall belong to a learned, knowledgeable person who is unnoticed and often unappreciated.

- Should Jia Wood happen to be present but Ding Fire absent from this Geng Metal Day Master's BaZi Chart, he or she may only lead an average life, at best.

- Where Ding Fire is present but Jia Wood absent, this Geng Metal Day Master person shall be a learned, knowledgeable leader, but lack of true wealth.

- Where Ding Fire and Jia Wood are both missing, however, this Geng Metal Day Master may lack a sense of purpose or direction in life.

- It must be emphasized, however, that the absence of Ding Fire would make it difficult for this Geng Metal Day Master to attain fame and recognition in life. Likewise, the absence of Jia Wood would make it difficult for this Geng Metal Day Master to have a sense of independence and achievements in life. Where either Ding Fire or Jia Wood is missing, this Geng Metal Day Master would only lead an average life, at best.

- Where Fire is missing from the chart, he or she may be afflicted by poverty or illness throughout his or her entire life. Any wealth this Day Master attains or accumulates would only be fleeting or unsustainable.

| Day Master | Geng 庚 Metal | | Month | Chen 辰 (Dragon) |

Additional Attributes

三月
Third Month

Dragon

格局 **Structural Star**	偏財 Indirect Wealth	正官 Direct Officer
用神 **Useful God**	Jia 甲 Wood	Ding 丁 Fire
Conditions	Where Jia Wood (Indirect Wealth Star) is present, this Geng Metal Day Master shall enjoy success in his or her career-related pursuits.	
Positive Circumstances	Ding Fire is also present in the Heavenly Stems.	
Negative Circumstances	Friend and Rob Wealth Stars penetrate through the Heavenly Stems.	

格局 **Structural Star**	偏財 Indirect Wealth	正財 Direct Wealth
用神 **Useful God**	Jia 甲 Wood	Yi 乙 Wood
Conditions	Where the Earthly Branches form a Wood (Wealth) formation – while Jia Wood and Yi Wood are also reveals in the Heavenly Stems, this Day Master shall prosper, although his or her wealth will not be lasting.	
Positive Circumstances	Geng Metal needs to be rooted. Fire element is present to forge Metal and unite the Wood.	
Negative Circumstances	Lack of roots for the Geng Metal.	

24

| Day Master | Geng 庚 Metal | | Month | Chen 辰 (Dragon) |

| | Additional Attributes | |

格局 Structural Star	七殺 Seven Killings	正官 Direct Officer
用神 Useful God	Bing 丙 Fire	Ding 丁 Fire
Conditions	Where the Earthly Branches encounter Bing Fire (Seven Killings Star) – Ren Water, (Eating God Star), must be seen penetrating through the Heavenly Stems.	
Positive Circumstances	Ren Water in the Heavenly Stems	
Negative Circumstances	Where Ren Water is either missing or not seen penetrating through the Heavenly Stems, this Geng Metal Day Master may be afflicted by a physical disability or chronic illness in life.	

* *Jia Wood and Ding Fire are the most-preferred Useful Gods for a Geng Metal Day Master born in a Chen (Dragon) Month.*

三月 Third Month

Dragon

25

| Day Master | Geng 庚 Metal | Month | Chen 辰 (Dragon) |

Summary

- Gui Water should preferably not penetrate through the Heavenly Stems unless the Earthly Branches is made of intense fire elements.

- Where Fire is missing from this Chart, he or she may be afflicted by poverty in life. Without Fire, Geng Metal will not shine.

- Where the Earthly Branches forms a Wealth Structure in the BaZi Chart – with Jia Wood also revealed in the Heavenly Stems – this Geng Metal Day Master shall prosper in life; although his or her wealth will not be lasting or sustainable.

- It would be preferable to use Ding Fire – instead of Bing Fire - as a Useful God, as far as this Geng Metal Day Master is concerned.

- Wu Earth – as an Indirect Resource Star – should not be used as it buries Metal.

Geng 庚 Metal Day Master, Born in Fourth Month 四月

Si 巳 (Snake) Month
May 6th - June 5th

Do note that the dates provided above are subject to slight yearly variations. Please refer to your Annual Tong Shu or Joey Yap's Ten Thousand Year Calendar for the accurate dates for each year.

Day Master Geng 庚 Metal　　　　**Month** Si 巳 (Snake)

日元 Day Master	月 Month
庚 *Geng* **Yang Metal**	巳 *Si* **Snake** **Yin Fire**

For a Geng Metal Day Master born in a Si (Snake) Month, a Seven Killings Structure is formed where Bing Fire is revealed as one of the Heavenly Stems.

Where Wu Earth is revealed as one of the Heavenly Stems, an Indirect Resource Structure is formed.

Where another Geng Metal is revealed as one of the Heavenly Stems, a Thriving Structure may be formed depending on the condition of the Earthly Branches.

Should, however, neither Bing Fire nor Wu Earth happen to be revealed within the Heavenly Stems, one should select a Structure according to the BaZi Chart's most prominent Qi attribute at one's discretion.

四月 Fourth Month

| Day Master | Geng 庚 Metal | Month | Si 巳 (Snake) |

庚金水喜用神提要 Regulating Useful God Reference Guide

月 Month	用神 Useful God			
4th Month 四月 Si 巳 (Snake) Month	壬 *Ren* **Yang Water**	戊 *Wu* **Yang Earth**	丙 *Bing* **Yang Fire**	丁 *Ding* **Yin Fire**

Snake

For a Si (Snake) Month, Ren Water, Wu Earth, Bing Fire and Ding Fire are the Regulating Useful Gods.

Bing Fire, however, cannot directly 'melt' or weaken Metal. As such, Ren Water remains the only feasible choice to control Metal.

Wu Earth is therefore the secondary Useful God, with Bing Fire as the 'intermediary' Useful God.

Where the Earthly Branches form a Metal Formation, Ding Fire is needed to transform from a weak to a strong and thriving one.

四月 Fourth Month

Snake

| Day Master | Geng 庚 Metal | | Month | Si 巳 (Snake) |

6th day of May – 5th day of June, Gregorian Calendar

Geng Metal is continuously produced and strengthened, although Fire is exceptionally strong in summer this month. Nevertheless, Metal would still be controlled by Fire, given the latter's strength in a Si (Snake) Month. As such, a Geng Metal Day Master born in a Si (Snake) Month would therefore have to be `moistened' by Water in order to grow.

The Si (Snake) Earthly Branch's Hidden Stems - Geng Metal and Wu Earth may also be treated as Useful Gods in certain cases. This is possible when there are roots for the Geng Metal day master.

Where Water is sufficiently present, Wood may be used in tandem with Water as Useful Gods.

And along with Water and Fire elements in the chart which are further produced and supported, this Geng Metal Day Master person shall prosper and become powerful and authoritative in life.

| Day Master | Geng 庚 Metal | Month | Si 巳 (Snake) |

Commentary

In addition to the preceding narratives on the potential Structures and scenarios resulting from a Geng Metal Day Master born in a Si (Snake) Month, the following circumstances also play their respective roles in determining the overall strength of this Day Master's BaZi Chart.

Note:

- Only Ren Water – as a Useful God – should be allowed to penetrate through the Heavenly Stems.

- Ding Fire should be prevented from combining with Ren Water to produce Wood, where possible

- Fire features prominently in a Si (Snake) Month. Where there is no Ren Water to penetrate through the Heavenly Stems, this Geng Metal Day Master may find it difficult to establish him or herself, where career-related pursuits are concerned.

- It would be best for Ding Fire to be avoided or at least prevented from penetrating through the Heavenly Stems. Where Ding Fire combines with Ren Water, any success this Geng Metal Day Master achieves in life may be overturned into failure; therefore causing him or her much disappointment and regret.

Snake

Day Master	Geng 庚 Metal		Month	Si 巳 (Snake)

Additional Attributes

格局 Structural Star	食神 Eating God	偏印 Indirect Resource	七殺 Seven Killings
用神 Useful God	Ren 壬 Water	Wu 戊 Earth	Bing 丙 Fire
Conditions	Where Ren Water, Wu Earth and Bing Fire are all present and co-exist harmoniously with one another in the BaZi Chart, this Geng Metal Day Master shall enjoy a successful and happy life. Where Bing Fire is missing, amongst all three elements, this Geng Metal Day Master's may not enjoy the same level of success and prosperity, compared to the preceding scenario.		
Positive Circumstances	Geng Metal being rooted.		
Negative Circumstances	Excessive fire in the Earthly Brances		

格局 Structural Star	七殺 Seven Killings
用神 Useful God	Bing 丙 Fire
Conditions	In a Seven Killing Structure, Metal should not be selected as Useful God.
Positive Circumstances	Ren Water appearing in the Heavenly Stems.
Negative Circumstances	In the absence of Ren Water, the person's quality of marriage will be very bad.

Day Master Geng 庚 Metal		Month Si 巳 (Snake)

Additional Attributes

Snake

格局 Structural Star	比肩 Friend	劫財 Rob Wealth
用神 Useful God	Geng 庚 Metal	Xin 辛 Metal
Conditions	Where the Earthly Branches form a Metal formation, only Ding Fire – the Direct Officer Star – may be used as a Useful God; and not Bing Fire – a Seven Killings Star.	
Positive Circumstances	Ding Fire in the Heavenly Stems. Rooted in the branches.	
Negative Circumstances	Ren Water and Gui Water will `hurt' Ding Fire (Direct Officer Star).	

* Ren Water and Wu Earth are the preferred Useful Gods.

** Bing Fire serves as the secondary Useful God in the Absence of Ding Fire to this Geng Metal Day Master.

Day Master	Geng 庚 Metal	Month	Si 巳 (Snake)

Summary

- Where a Seven Killings structure is formed the presence of a Goat Blade Star (Rob Wealth Star) would propel or drive this Seven Killings Structure towards producing an extremely volatile Day Master. Hence it is undesirable. Best to have Ren Water (Eating God Star) – controlling the Seven Killings. This would produce a far more powerful Geng Metal Day Master.

- Where the Earthly Branches meet with You (Rooster), forming a Goat Blade formation with this Geng Metal Day Master, a Seven Killings Star in the Heavenly Stems would be undesirable. Instead, Ding Fire the Direct Officer Star , should be used to maintain balance in the BaZi Chart. It is also important to avoid having Gui Water (Hurting Officer Star) – penetrating through the Heavenly Stems.

- Geng Metal Day Master would also fare better, when entering a West (Autumn Metal) or North (Winter Water) Luck Cycles. It would be unfavorable and unsuitable for this Geng Metal Day Master to enter a Fire Luck Period.

- The presence of Ren Water (Eating God Star) would strengthen the wood (Wealth) stars.

- Where Wu Earth (Indirect Resource Star) – penetrates through the Heavenly Stems, however, it would result in a `wedge' or `separation' taking place between Water and Wood.

Geng 庚 Metal Day Master, Born in Fifth Month 五月

Wu 午 (Horse) Month
June 6 - July 6th

Do note that the dates provided above are subject to slight yearly variations. Please refer to your Annual Tong Shu or Joey Yap's Ten Thousand Year Calendar for the accurate dates for each year.

五月

Fifth Month

Horse

Day Master Geng 庚 Metal   **Month** Wu 午 (Horse)

日元 **Day Master**	月 **Month**
庚 *Geng* **Yang Metal**	午 *Wu* **Horse** **Yang Fire**

For a Geng Metal Day Master born in a Wu (Horse) Month, a Direct Officer Structure is formed where Ding Fire is revealed as one of the Heavenly Stems.

Where Ji Earth is revealed as one of the Heavenly Stems, a Direct Resource Structure is formed.

Should, however, neither Ding Fire nor Ji Earth happen to be revealed within the Heavenly Stems, one should select a Structure according to the BaZi Chart's most prominent Qi attribute at one's discretion.

Day Master	Geng 庚 Metal		Month	Wu 午 (Horse)

庚金水喜用神提要 Regulating Useful God Reference Guide

月 Month	用神 Useful God	
5th Month 五月 **Wu 午 (Horse) Month**	壬 *Ren* **Yang Water**	癸 *Gui* **Yin Water**

Horse

For a Wu (Horse) Month, Ren Water and Gui Water are the Regulating Useful Gods.

Priority should be given to Ren Water, as the primary Useful God; with Gui Water serving as the secondary Useful God. Where possible, the Earthly Branches should also see Geng Metal and Xin Metal, since both play the roles of supporting auxiliary Useful Gods as well.

In the absence of Ren Water and Gui Water, Wu Earth and Ji Earth may be used to weaken and hence keep Fire Qi under control.

五月 Fifth Month

五
月

Fifth Month

Horse

Day Master	Geng 庚 Metal	Month	Wu 午 (Horse)

6th day of June – 6th day of July, Gregorian Calendar

Earth and Fire feature prominently in a Wu (Horse) Month. Earth is `dry' and Fire is exceptionally hot in summer. Without Water, it would be difficult – if not downright impossible – for Metal to be produced and hence strengthened.

Where Fire - in a Wu (Horse) Month – meets with more Wood, the latter will support and assist the former to `burn' and `blaze' even more. Metal should hence be rooted in Earth that is `moistened' by Water, in order to remain well-balanced. The presence of `dry' or `parched' Earth alone would be insufficient to produce and strengthen this Geng Metal Day Master.

Obviously, this Geng Metal Day Master should also avoid meeting more Wood and Fire stars as much as possible, in order to prevent Geng Metal from being `melted away' by extremely strong Fire.

Water, present in abundance, would be able to alleviate this Geng Metal Day Master's predicament, by `moistening' Earth. If this is possible, this Geng Metal Day Master shall belong to a very intelligent and remarkable achiever. Success would come through his/her literary and creative prowess.

Day Master	Geng 庚 Metal	Month	Wu 午 (Horse)

Commentary

五
月

Fifth Month

Horse

In addition to the preceding narratives on the potential Structures and scenarios resulting from a Geng Metal Day Master born in a Wu (Horse) Month, the following circumstances also play their respective roles in determining the overall strength of this Day Master's BaZi Chart.

Note:

- Ren Water is this Geng Metal Day Master's preferred Useful God this month.

- Wu Earth and Ji Earth should be avoided or at least prevented from penetrating through the Heavenly Stems.

- In order to bring balance to a Geng Metal Day Master born in a Wu (Horse) Month, Ren Water must be able to penetrate through the Heavenly Stems. In addition, Wu Earth and Ji Earth should also be prevented from penetrating through the Heavenly Stems. This is because both Earth elements have the potential to `contaminate' Ren Water and if this is the case, this Geng Metal Day Master would only be able to lead an average life, at best.

- Where the Heavenly Stems and Earthly Branches form a Fire Structure, this Geng Metal may be compelled to slog and toil for a living. Where Ren Water or Gui Water is seen penetrating through the Heavenly Stems, however, this Geng Metal Day Master may enjoy unexpected success or outcomes in life.

- Where Wu Earth and Ji Earth are seen penetrating through the Heavenly Stems, this Geng Metal Day Master may be afflicted by loneliness as well as poverty in life.

Day Master	Geng 庚 Metal		Month	Wu 午 (Horse)

Additional Attributes

格局 Structural Star	食神 Eating God	比肩 Friend	傷官 Hurting Officer
用神 Useful God	Ren 壬 Water	Geng 庚 Metal	Gui 癸 Water
Conditions	Where Ren Water, Geng Metal and Gui Water are all present in the Heavenly Stems of this BaZi Chart, this person shall certainly enjoy great fortune and prosperity in life.		
Positive Circumstances	Where Wu Earth or Ji Earth is present, Jia Wood is needed to keep either under control.		
Negative Circumstances	If Wu Earth or Ji Earth penetrates through the Heavenly Stems, the entire structure of the BaZi Chart would be upset and 'ruined'.		

格局 Structural Star	七殺 Seven Killings	正官 Direct Officer
用神 Useful God	Bing 丙 Fire	Ding 丁 Fire
Conditions	Where the Earthly Branches forms Fire structure – and neither Ren Water, Gui Water or Geng Metal is seen penetrating through the Heavenly Stems – the person will be afflicted by poverty throughout his or her entire life.	
Positive Circumstances	Ren is revealed in the Heavenly Stems.	
Negative Circumstances	Where Ren Water and Gui Water are present – and Wu Earth or Ji Earth as Resource Stars also happen to be revealed – this Geng Metal Day Master may only lead an average life.	

Day Master	Geng 庚 Metal		Month	Wu 午 (Horse)

Additional Attributes

格局 Structural Star	偏財 Indirect Wealth	七殺 Seven Killings
用神 Useful God	Jia 甲 Wood	Bing 丙 Fire
Conditions	Where Wood and Fire are all over the chart – while Companion and Resource Stars are totally absent – a Follow the Leader Structure maybe formed. Under such circumstances, this Geng Metal Day Master shall enjoy great success and fame in life. This is a special structure.	
Positive Circumstances	Fire and Wood stars in the Heavenly Stems and Branches.	
Negative Circumstances	Presence of Water and Metal Stars.	

Horse

* *Ren Water is the primary or preferred Useful God, while Gui Water is the secondary Useful God.*

** *The Resource Stars of Wu Earth and Ji Earth should not penetrate through the Heavenly Stems.*

五
月

Fifth Month

| Day Master | Geng 庚 Metal | Month | Wu 午 (Horse) |

Summary

- The absence of Water in a Wu (Horse) Month would only result in this Day Master's BaZi Chart having a substandard structure.

- In the absence of Water, Ji Earth may be alternatively used to weaken and keep Fire under control. This Geng Metal Day Master shall, of course, prosper when entering a Water Luck Period, as well as enjoy the good quality of life in the latter (older) stages of his or her life.

Horse

Wei 未 (Goat) Month
July 7th - August 7th

Do note that the dates provided above are subject to slight yearly variations. Please refer to your Annual Tong Shu or Joey Yap's Ten Thousand Year Calendar for the accurate dates for each year.

BaZi Structures & Structural Useful Gods 格局與格局用神

| Day Master | Geng 庚 Metal | Month | Wei 未 (Goat) |

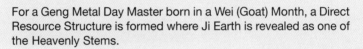

日元 **Day Master**	月 **Month**
庚 *Geng* **Yang Metal**	未 *Wei* **Goat** **Yin Earth**

For a Geng Metal Day Master born in a Wei (Goat) Month, a Direct Resource Structure is formed where Ji Earth is revealed as one of the Heavenly Stems.

Where Yi Wood is revealed as one of the Heavenly Stems, a Direct Wealth Structure is formed.

Where Ding Fire is revealed as one of the Heavenly Stems, a Direct Officer Structure is formed.

Should, however, neither Yi Wood nor Ji Earth nor Ding Fire happen to be revealed within the Heavenly Stems, one should select a Structure according to the BaZi Chart's most prominent Qi attribute at one's discretion.

Day Master	Geng 庚 Metal	Month	Wei 未 (Goat)

庚金水喜用神提要 Regulating Useful God Reference Guide

Goat

月 Month	用神 Useful God	
6th Month 六月 **Wei 未 (Goat) Month**	丁 *Ding* **Yin Fire**	甲 *Jia* **Yang Wood**

For a Wei (Goat) Month, Ding Fire and Jia Wood are the Regulating Useful Gods.

Where the Earthly Branches encounter an Earth Formation, Jia Wood would be the primary or first-choice Useful God, with Ding Fire serving as the secondary Useful God.

45

Day Master	Geng 庚 Metal	Month	Wei 未 (Goat)

7th day of July – 7th day of August, Gregorian Calendar

Fire and Earth stars are very strong in a Wei (Goat) Month. Earth would inevitably be `leaden' and `parched'.

As such, Water as a Useful God should first be used to `moisten' Earth. Meanwhile, Wood may simultaneously be used to `loosen' Earth. If this scenario is attainable, this Geng Metal Day Master shall prosper and become wealthy his or her entire life.

Goat

Water and Wood stars are easily the most important Useful Gods for a Geng Metal Day Master born in a Wei (Goat) Month.

In the case of a Geng Metal Day Master born in an hour where Metal and Water stars are dominant, Wood Qi would be weak or weakened in the presence of abundant Metal Qi. Under such circumstances, however, an abundance of Water would allow Wood (which is the Wealth Star to Geng) - to be supported by its resource, thereby allowing this Geng Metal Day Master to prosper in life.

| Day Master | Geng 庚 Metal | Month | Wei 未 (Goat) |

Commentary

In addition to the preceding narratives on the potential Structures and scenarios resulting from a Geng Metal Day Master born in a Wei (Goat) Month, the following circumstances also play their respective roles in determining the overall strength of this Day Master's BaZi Chart.

Goat

Note:

- Where Jia Wood – a Wealth Star - is revealed in the BaZi Chart but Ding Fire is not, this Geng Metal Day Master may do well as petty-trader or modest entrepreneur.

- Where Ding Fire is revealed but Jia Wood is not, this Geng Metal Day Master may only lead an average life, at best.

- Where two Ding Fire and two Geng Metal elements penetrate through the Heavenly Stems, this Geng Metal Day Master shall be a knowledgeable and scholarly person, who will also do well in an administrative or managerial position in life.

- Where Ren Water penetrates to the Heavenly Stem, there will be many opportunities in life.

六月
Sixth Month

Goat

| **Day Master** | **Geng 庚 Metal** | **Month** | **Wei 未 (Goat)** |

Additional Attributes

格局 **Structural Star**	正官 Direct Officer	偏財 Indirect Wealth
用神 **Useful God**	Ding 丁 Fire	Jia 甲 Wood
Conditions	Where both Ding Fire and Jia Wood are present in the Heavenly Stems of the BaZi Chart, this person is likely to enjoy a life of great financial success.	
Positive Circumstances	Presence of wet earth element in the Earthly Branches	
Negative Circumstances	Gui Water – a Hurting Officer Star – penetrates through the Heavenly Stems.	

Day Master	Geng 庚 Metal		Month	Wei 未 (Goat)

Additional Attributes

格局 **Structural Star**	偏印 Indirect Resource	正印 Direct Resource
用神 **Useful God**	Wu 戊 Earth	Ji 己 Earth
Conditions	Where the Four Graveyard Earthly Branches of Chen (Dragon), Xu (Dog), Chou (Ox) and Wei (Goat) happen to be present at the same time, Jia Wood would be the primary Useful God, with Ding Fire the secondary Useful God.	
Positive Circumstances	Absence of Earth element at the Heavenly Stems	
Negative Circumstances	Ji Earth next to Jia Wood would render this formation useless.	

六月

Sixth Month

Goat

49

六
月
Sixth Month

Goat

Day Master Geng 庚 Metal   **Month** Wei 未 (Goat)

Summary

- Gui Water (Hurting Officer Star) – should be prevented from penetrating through the Heavenly Stems.

- Where Water – as Eating God and Hurting Officer Stars – is absent to produce Wood – which are Wealth Stars – the overall structure of this Geng Metal Day Master's BaZi Chart would be a substandard one.

- Where Ding Fire and Jia Wood are both missing from the BaZi Chart, any structure formed would still be a substandard one.

- As far as Wood is concerned, only Jia Wood would allow this Geng Metal Day Master to excel in life. In its absence, Yi Wood would not be able to substitute Jia Wood as a Useful God, in bringing about a similar outcome.

- As far as Fire is concerned, only Ding Fire - as a Useful God - would allow this Geng Metal Day Master to prosper in life. In its absence, Bing Fire would not be able to substitute Ding Fire as a Useful God, in bringing about a similar outcome.

Geng 庚 Metal Day Master, Born in Seventh Month 七月

Shen 申 (Monkey) Month
August 8th - September 7th

Do note that the dates provided above are subject to slight yearly variations. Please refer to your Annual Tong Shu or Joey Yap's Ten Thousand Year Calendar for the accurate dates for each year.

Day Master Geng 庚 Metal   **Month** Shen 申 (Monkey)

日元 **Day Master**	月 **Month**
庚 *Geng* **Yang Metal**	申 *Shen* **Monkey** **Yang Metal**

In the case of a Geng Metal Day Master born in a Shen (Monkey) Month, the Shen (Monkey) Earthly Branch is also Geng Metal's `Prosperous' position.

A Thriving Structure is to be formed, especially when Geng Metal Qi is prosperous.

Where Wu Earth is revealed as one of the Heavenly Stems, an Indirect Resource Structure is formed.

Where Ren Water is revealed as one of the Heavenly Stems, a Eating God Structure is formed.

| Day Master | Geng 庚 Metal | Month | Shen 申 (Monkey) |

庚金水喜用神提要 **Regulating Useful God Reference Guide**

月 Month	用神 Useful God	
7th Month 七月 **Shen 申 (Monkey) Month**	丁 *Ding* **Yin Fire**	甲 *Jia* **Yang Wood**

Monkey

For a Shen (Monkey) Month, Ding Fire and Jia Wood are the Regulating Useful Gods.

Priority should be accorded Ding Fire as a primary Useful God, with Jia Wood being used to 'guide' and ensure the continuity of Ding Fire.

BaZi Structures & Structural Useful Gods 格局與格局用神

Day Master	Geng 庚 Metal	Month	Shen 申 (Monkey)

8th day of August – 7th day of September, Gregorian Calendar

`Prosperous' Star feature prominently in the case of a Geng Metal Day Master born in a Shen (Monkey) Month. Metal and Water stars are strong this month. This is because Metal Qi is at its peak in autumn.

When Wood is selected as the Useful God – presence of Water to produce and further strengthen Wood is desirable. This enables the Geng Metal Day Master to enjoy long lasting prosperity.

Monkey

Day Master	Geng 庚 Metal		Month	Shen 申 (Monkey)

Commentary

In addition to the preceding narratives on the potential Structures and scenarios resulting from a Geng Metal Day Master born in a Shen (Monkey) Month, the following circumstances also play their respective roles in determining the overall strength of this Day Master's BaZi Chart.

Note:

- Ding Fire and Jia Wood should both be present in the BaZi Chart.

- Where the Earthly Branches form a Fire Structure; this Geng Metal Day Master shall be blessed with extraordinary fortune and achievements in life.

- Where the Earthly Branches form an Earth Structure, Jia Wood should be selected as the primary Useful God, with Ding Fire serving as the secondary Useful God. Under such circumstances, this Geng Metal Day Master shall also become immensely wealthy in life.

- Where the Earthly Branches form a Water Structure – with three Geng Metal elements penetrating through the Heavenly Stems – the person may enjoy tremendous support and recognition for his ideas and knowledge.

七
月
Seventh Month

Monkey

55

Day Master Geng 庚 Metal		**Month** Shen 申 (Monkey)

Additional Attributes

格局 **Structural Star**	正官 Direct Officer	偏財 Indirect Wealth
用神 **Useful God**	Ding 丁 Fire	Jia 甲 Wood
Conditions	A Geng Metal Day Master with both Ding Fire and Jia Wood present in his or her BaZi Chart can enjoy an extraordinary life, full of success and prosperity.	
Positive Circumstances	Ding Fire and Jia Wood rooted in the Branches.	
Negative Circumstances	In the absence of Jia Wood, Gui Water (Hurting Officer Star) should be avoided as it extinguishes Ding Fire.	

Monkey

格局 **Structural Star**	偏財 Indirect Wealth	正財 Direct Wealth
用神 **Useful God**	Jia 甲 Wood	Yi 乙 Wood
Conditions	Without Ding Fire, the presence of Jia Wood and Yi Wood merely forms a mediocre Wealth Structure	
Positive Circumstances	Presence of Ding Fire will ensure long term success and fame.	
Negative Circumstances	Absence of Ding Fire.	

Day Master	Geng 庚 Metal	Month	Shen 申 (Monkey)

Additional Attributes

格局 **Structural Star**	食神 Eating God	傷官 Hurting Officer
用神 **Useful God**	Ren 壬 Water	Gui 癸 Water
Conditions	Where the Earthly Branches forms the Water Formation (Output Elements) and there is no Jia Wood in the chart – this person is not very intelligent. His/her life is full of missed opportunities.	
Positive Circumstances	Presence of Jia Wood.	
Negative Circumstances	Jia Wood is completely absent from the BaZi Chart.	

*   *Ding Fire and Jia Wood are the preferred Useful Gods for this Geng Metal Day Master.*

| Day Master | Geng 庚 Metal | Month | Shen 申 (Monkey) |

Monkey

Summary

- Where three Geng Metal elements happen to be present in the Heavenly Stems of a Geng Metal Day Master born in a Shen (Monkey) Month's BaZi Chart – with the Earthly Branches also forming a Water Structure – a situation known as a 'Well-Gate Blocking' (井欄叉) takes place. Together with the presence of Jia and Yi Wood, this is a fabulous chart belong to successful business people. Going through Wood Luck Cycles would be even more desirable.

- Where the Earthly Branches form a Water Structure - with an abundance of Geng Metal, as well as Bing Fire and Ding Fire found in the Heavenly Stems – need the help of Jia Wood or Yi Wood (Wealth Stars) to bring out all the latent talents in the chart.

Geng 庚 Metal Day Master, Born in Eighth Month 八月

You 酉 (Rooster) Month
September 8th - October 7th

Do note that the dates provided above are subject to slight yearly variations. Please refer to your Annual Tong Shu or Joey Yap's Ten Thousand Year Calendar for the accurate dates for each year.

| Day Master Geng 庚 Metal | Month You 酉 (Rooster) |

日元 **Day Master**	月 **Month**
庚 *Geng* **Yang Metal**	酉 *You* **Rooster** **Yin Metal**

For a Geng Metal Day Master born in a You (Rooster) Month, the Earthly Branch of You (Rooster) is Geng Metal's Rob Wealth, which also forms a Goat Blade Structure with this Geng Metal Day Master.

| Day Master | Geng 庚 Metal | Month | You 酉 (Rooster) |

庚金水喜用神提要 Regulating Useful God Reference Guide

Rooster

月 Month	用神 Useful God
8th Month 八月 **You 酉 (Rooster) Month**	丁 *Ding* **Yin Fire**　　甲 *Jia* **Yang Wood**　　丙 *Bing* **Yang Fire**

For a You (Rooster) Month, Ding Fire, Jia Wood and Bing Fire are the Regulating Useful Gods.

Ding Fire and Jia Wood should be selected as Useful Gods, in beautifying this Geng Metal Day Master. Bing Fire serves as an 'arbitrator' in 'adjusting' the 'weather' or Qi of this Geng Metal Day Master's BaZi Chart, in ensuring that it remains well-balanced.

八月

Eighth Month

酉
Rooster

| Day Master | Geng 庚 Metal | | Month | You 酉 (Rooster) |

8th day of August – 7th day of September, Gregorian Calendar

Metal is at its peak or strongest in autumn, as in the case of a Geng Metal Day Master born in a You (Rooster) Month.

Since Metal is strong in autumn, Wood will be weakened in this time. As such, Fire is needed to keep such strong Metal under control.

Where Fire is present but Wood absent, this Geng Metal Day Master may lack wealth capacity, no matter how powerful or authoritative he or she may be in life. Indeed, any position or status held by this Day Master in life would also be fleeting or unsustainable.

If both Water and Wood stars are present, this Geng Metal Day Master shall prosper and become wealthy, powerful and authoritative in life. Where Wood Qi exceeds Water Qi, this person may even become extraordinarily wealthy in life.

| Day Master | Geng 庚 Metal | Month | You 酉 (Rooster) |

Commentary

In addition to the preceding narratives on the potential Structures and scenarios resulting from a Geng Metal Day Master born in a You (Rooster) Month, the following circumstances also play their respective roles in determining the overall strength of this Day Master's BaZi Chart.

Note :

- Bing Fire and Ding Fire are the preferred Useful Gods for a Geng Metal Day Master born in a You (Rooster) Month, with Jia Wood serving as a supporting or auxiliary Useful God.

- A Geng Metal Day Master born in a You (Rooster) Month forms a Goat Blade Structure. Under such circumstances, Bing Fire and Ding Fire must be present as Useful Gods for this Geng Metal Day Master.

- Where Ding Fire, Jia Wood and Bing Fire are all revealed, this Geng Metal Day Master shall enjoy success in his or her life's pursuits.

八月 Eighth Month

Rooster

| Day Master | Geng 庚 Metal | Month | You 酉 (Rooster) |

Additional Attributes

格局 **Structural Star**	七殺 Seven Killings
用神 **Useful God**	Bing 丙 Fire
Conditions	Where only Bing Fire – a Seven Killings Star – is employed as a Useful God, this Geng Metal Day Master may find it difficult to prosper in life, no matter how attractive or appealing he or she may be.
Positive Circumstances	At least one Ding Fire element should be present, although this Geng Metal Day Master's Direct Officer and Seven Killings Stars should not intermingle freely with one another.
Negative Circumstances	Ren Water and Gui Water penetrate through the Heavenly Stems.

八月

Eighth Month

Rooster

Day Master Geng 庚 Metal		**Month** You 酉 (Rooster)

Additional Attributes

格局 **Structural Star**	比肩 Friend	劫財 Rob Wealth
用神 **Useful God**	Geng 庚 Metal	Ren 壬 Water
Conditions	Where the Earthly Branches meets with more Metal Qi, the simultaneous presence of Water would result in a Follow the Leader Structure being formed.	
Positive Circumstances	Water must be present in the BaZi Chart, since its absence would not allow a Follow the Leader Structure to be formed.	
Negative Circumstances	It would be unfavourable to this Geng Metal Day Master, should he or she enter a Fire Luck Period.	

Rooster

* *The You (Rooster) Earthly Branch should not meet a clash. Clashing the Goat Blade may be a disastrous structure.*

** *Bing Fire and Ding Fire should be simultaneously employed as preferred Useful Gods, but positioned in different positions.*

| Day Master | Geng 庚 Metal | Month | You 酉 (Rooster) |

Rooster

Summary

- Where the Yi Wood, Bing Fire and Ding Fire all appear in the Heavenly Stem of this chart, it is known as a special formation known as the Three Wonder Noble. It is extra special in this month's condition.

- The Three Wonder Noble can also be found in the Branches in the form of Mao (Rabbit), Si (Snake), Wu (Horse).

- Where there is an abundance of Jia Wood and Yi Wood as Wealth Stars – but Bing Fire and Ding Fire are missing – this Geng Metal Day Master shall possess an artistic or creative flair but no real wealth.

- Direct Officer and Seven Killings are used together only in this month for this Day Master.

Geng 庚 Metal Day Master, Born in Ninth Month 九月

Xu 戌 (Dog) Month
October 8th - November 6th

Do note that the dates provided above are subject to slight yearly variations. Please refer to your Annual Tong Shu or Joey Yap's Ten Thousand Year Calendar for the accurate dates for each year.

戌
Dog

日元 **Day Master**	月 **Month**
庚 *Geng* **Yang Metal**	戌 *Xu* **Dog** **Yang Earth**

Day Master Geng 庚 Metal

Month Xu 戌 (Dog)

For a Geng Metal Day Master born in a Xu (Dog) Month, an Indirect Resource Structure is formed where Wu Earth is revealed as one of the Heavenly Stems.

Where Ding Fire is revealed as one of the Heavenly Stems, a Direct Officer Structure is formed.

Should, however, neither Ding Fire nor Wu Earth happen to be revealed within the Heavenly Stems, one should select a Structure according to the BaZi Chart's most prominent Qi attribute at one's discretion.

| Day Master | Geng 庚 Metal | Month | Xu 戌 (Dog) |

庚金水喜用神提要 Regulating Useful God Reference Guide

Dog

月 Month	用神 Useful God	
9th Month 九月 **Xu 戌 (Dog) Month**	甲 *Jia* **Yang Wood**	壬 *Ren* **Yang Water**

For a Xu (Dog) Month, Jia Wood and Ren Water are the Regulating Useful Gods.

Where Earth is 'thick' or 'leaden' in a Xu (Dog) Month, Jia Wood may be used to 'loosen' it. Ren Water may then be employed as the secondary Useful God, to 'cleanse' this Geng Metal Day Master.

A Geng Metal Day Master born in a Xu (Dog) Month should avoid meeting Ji Earth, which could only 'contaminate' Ren Water.

| Day Master | Geng 庚 Metal | | Month | Xu 戌 (Dog) |

8th day of October – 7th day of November, Gregorian Calendar

Although Earth and Metal are strong in a Xu (Dog) Month, Earth is invariably 'leaden' and 'thick' in the autumn, while both Earth and Metal are also 'dry' at this time of the year.

Water should hence be used as the primary Useful God, in tandem with Wood as the secondary Useful God to 'loosen' Earth. Where Water Qi is weak or lacking while Earth is 'thick' and 'leaden', the Wood Qi would tend to be more 'brittle' and weaker.

It would also be preferable for a this chart to avoid meeting additional, excessive Earth stars, since Metal would invariably be 'buried' under 'thick', 'leaden' Earth.

Where possible, there should not be an abundance of Fire Qi as well, as Fire does have the propensity to produce and hence further strengthen Earth, which would also be 'parched' and 'leaden'.

Dog

九
月
Ninth Month

| Day Master | Geng 庚 Metal | Month | Xu 戌 (Dog) |

Commentary

In addition to the preceding narratives on the potential Structures and scenarios resulting from a Geng Metal Day Master born in a Xu (Dog) Month, the following circumstances also play their respective roles in determining the overall strength of this Day Master's BaZi Chart.

Note:

- Jia Wood and Ren Water are the preferred Useful Gods.

- Where possible, Ji Earth should be prevented from penetrating through the Heavenly Stems.

- Where the Earthly Branches form a Fire Structure – while Ren Water is revealed in the Heavenly Stems – this chart belongs to a highly capable leader, well respected and admired in his/her life.

- Ji Earth should not be allowed to penetrate through the Heavenly Stems, since it will weaken and adversely affect Jia Wood and contaminate Ren Water, which are this Geng Metal Day Master's most important Useful Gods.

九
月

Ninth Month

Dog

Day Master	Geng 庚 Metal	Month	Xu 戌 (Dog)

Additional Attributes

格局 Structural Star	偏財 Indirect Wealth	食神 Eating God
用神 Useful God	Jia 甲 Wood	Ren 壬 Water
Conditions	Where Jia Wood and Ren Water appears at the same time, there will be life of great achievements. Should Wu Earth and Ji Earth (Resource Stars) – penetrate through the Heavenly Stems, life may be difficult and success is unaatainable.	
Positive Circumstances	Where Wu Earth and Ji Earth are seen in the BaZi Chart, two Jia Wood Heavenly Stems must at least be present, to counter and negate any ill-effects brought about by these Resource Stars.	
Negative Circumstances	Wu Earth and Ji Earth penetrate through the Heavenly Stems.	

Day Master	Geng 庚 Metal	Month	Xu 戌 (Dog)

九月 Ninth Month

戌 Dog

Additional Attributes

格局 **Structural Star**	七殺 Seven Killings
用神 **Useful God**	Bing 丙 Fire
Conditions	Where the Earthly Branches form a Fire Structure – and Ren Water is also present in the Heavenly Stems – this Geng Metal Day Master shall enjoy a happy and prosperous life.
Positive Circumstances	Ren Water should, preferably, penetrate through the Heavenly Stems.
Negative Circumstances	Ren Water does not penetrate through the Heavenly Stems.

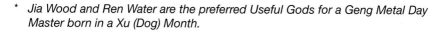

* *Jia Wood and Ren Water are the preferred Useful Gods for a Geng Metal Day Master born in a Xu (Dog) Month.*

** *Ji Earth should not be revealed in the Heavenly Stems.*

| Day Master | Geng 庚 Metal | Month | Xu 戌 (Dog) |

Summary

- Where Ren Water is revealed in the Heavenly Stems of the BaZi Chart , there will be success in life.

- Wu Earth and Ji Earth should not be seen penetrating through the Heavenly Stems. Otherwise, two Jia Wood elements would be needed to penetrate through the Heavenly Stems, in order to counter and negate the ill-effects brought about by both these Resource Stars.

- Yi Wood (Wealth Star) – would be of no use to this Geng Metal Day Master, as a Useful God.

- Where Ren Water and Jia Wood are absent from the BaZi Chart of this Geng Metal Day Master, any structure formed therein would still be regarded as a substandard one.

Geng 庚 Metal Day Master, Born in Tenth Month 十月

Hai 亥 (Pig) Month
November 7th - December 6th

Do note that the dates provided above are subject to slight yearly variations. Please refer to your Annual Tong Shu or Joey Yap's Ten Thousand Year Calendar for the accurate dates for each year.

Day Master Geng 庚 Metal　　　　**Month** Hai 亥 (Pig)

十月 Tenth Month

Pig

日元 **Day Master**	月 **Month**
庚 *Geng* **Yang Metal**	亥 *Hai* **Pig** **Yin Water**

For a Geng Metal Day Master born in a Hai (Pig) Month, an Eating God Structure is formed where Ren Water is revealed as one of the Heavenly Stems.

Where Jia Wood is revealed as one of the Heavenly Stems, an Indirect Wealth Structure is formed.

Should, however, neither Ren Water nor Jia Wood happen to be revealed within the Heavenly Stems, one should select a Structure according to the BaZi Chart's most prominent Qi attribute at one's discretion.

Day Master	Geng 庚 Metal	Month	Hai 亥 (Pig)

庚金水喜用神提要 Regulating Useful God Reference Guide

亥 Pig

月 Month	用神 Useful God
10th Month 十月 **Hai 亥 (Pig) Month**	丁 *Ding* **Yin Fire** 丙 *Bing* **Yang Fire**

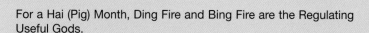

For a Hai (Pig) Month, Ding Fire and Bing Fire are the Regulating Useful Gods.

Since Water and Metal Qi are both invariably `cold' in a Hai (Pig) Month, it would be preferable for these elements to encounter or be exposed to Bing Fire or Ding Fire, as Useful Gods.

Jia Wood would, however, also be needed to produce and hence ensure that Ding Fire remains strong in a Hai (Pig) Month.

Pig

Day Master Geng 庚 Metal   **Month** Hai 亥 (Pig)

7th day of November – 6th day of December, Gregorian Calendar

Naturally, the Qi of this Day Master's BaZi Chart would be rather chilly, with Earth Qi extremely weak in winter.

Should there be insufficient Fire, however, it would be difficult for Earth to be 'warmed' or kept 'warm' in winter. As such, the presence of Fire in itself would suffice to 'warm' Metal, Earth and Wood. Without Fire, non of the other elements - Metal, Earth and Wood may then serve as Useful Gods for this Geng Metal Day Master.

A Geng Metal Day Master born in a Hai (Pig) Month needs 'warm' Earth, as its first-choice or primary Useful God. This is because such Earth would allow Metal Qi to be further strengthened, while simultaneously keeping Water Qi – which is already strong in winter – under control.

Day Master	Geng 庚 Metal		Month	Hai 亥 (Pig)

Commentary

十月

Tenth Month

Pig

In addition to the preceding narratives on the potential Structures and scenarios resulting from a Geng Metal Day Master born in a Hai (Pig) Month, the following circumstances also play their respective roles in determining the overall strength of this Day Master's BaZi Chart.

Note:

- Only Bing Fire and Ding Fire may be used as Regulating Useful Gods, in 'adjusting' the 'weather' and hence Qi of the BaZi Chart of a Geng Metal Day Master born in a Hai (Pig) Month.

- The absence of Bing Fire and Ding Fire from the BaZi would make it difficult – if not downright impossible – for this Day Master's Hurting Officer Stars to produce Wealth Stars.

- Where Bing Fire or Ding Fire is revealed in the chart, this Geng Metal Day Master shall enjoy much success in his or her career.

- Where the Earthly Branches form a Water Structure – but Bing Fire and Ding Fire do not penetrate through the Heavenly Stems – the overall structure of this Geng Metal Day Master's BaZi Chart would still be a substandard one.

- Where Bing Fire and Jia Wood are both revealed in the Heavenly Stems – but Ding Fire remains missing – this Geng Metal Day Master would only be able to lead an average life, at best.

十月 Tenth Month

亥 Pig

Day Master Geng 庚 Metal		**Month** Hai 亥 (Pig)
Additional Attributes		

格局 **Structural Star**	正官 Direct Officer	七殺 Seven Killings
用神 **Useful God**	Ding 丁 Fire	Bing 丙 Fire
Conditions	Where Ding Fire and Bing Fire are both revealed in the Heavenly Stems, this person shall be blessed with fame, as well as enjoy immense success in his or her career.	
Positive Circumstances	The Earthly Branches of Wu (Horse), Yin (Tiger) and Si (Snake) – which all contain either Ding Fire or Bing Fire in their Hidden Stems – are present in this Geng Metal Day Master's BaZi Chart.	
Negative Circumstances	Presence Gui Water to extinguish the Ding Fire and block the Bing Fire.	

Day Master	Geng 庚 Metal	Month	Hai 亥 (Pig)

Additional Attributes

格局 **Structural Star**	偏財 Indirect Wealth
用神 **Useful God**	Jia 甲 Wood
Conditions	Where a Wealth Structure is formed but Ding Fire is missing, this Geng Metal Day Master may only lead an average life, at best.
Positive Circumstances	Ding Fire must be present.
Negative Circumstances	Ding Present but combining with Ren Water.

亥 Pig

* *Ding Fire and Bing Fire are the preferred Useful Gods for a Geng Metal Day Master born in a Hai (Pig) Month.*

| Day Master | Geng 庚 Metal | | Month | Hai 亥 (Pig) |

Summary

- In the absence of Ding Fire and Bing Fire from the BaZi Chart, any other structure that may be formed would still be a substandard one. Furthermore, this Geng Metal Day Master may also be afflicted by loneliness in life.

- Ding Fire is the most important and hence primary Useful God for this Geng Metal Day Master. It would still be `acceptable' for Bing Fire and Jia Wood to be missing from this Geng Metal Day Master's BaZi Chart; but Ding Fire must however be present under any circumstance.

- Where Bing Fire and Jia Wood are revealed in the Heavenly Stems – but Ding Fire is not – this Geng Metal Day Master would only get to lead an average life, at best.

Pig

Geng 庚 Metal Day Master, Born in Eleventh Month 十一月

Zi 子 (Rat) Month
December 7th - January 5th

Do note that the dates provided above are subject to slight yearly variations. Please refer to your Annual Tong Shu or Joey Yap's Ten Thousand Year Calendar for the accurate dates for each year.

| Day Master | Geng 庚 Metal | | Month | Zi 子 (Rat) |

日元 Day Master	月 Month
庚 *Geng* **Yang Metal**	子 *Zi* **Rat** **Yang Water**

For a Geng Metal Day Master born in a Zi (Rat) Month, a Hurting Officer Structure is formed where Gui Water is revealed as a Heavenly Stem.

Even if Gui Water is not revealed as a Heavenly Stem, a Hurting Officer Structure would still be considered to have been formed.

| Day Master | Geng 庚 Metal | Month | Zi 子 (Rat) |

庚金水喜用神提要 **Regulating Useful God Reference Guide**

月 **Month**	用神 **Useful God**
11th Month 十一月 Zi 子 (Rat) Month	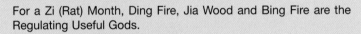丁 *Ding* **Yin Fire**　　甲 *Jia* **Yang Wood**　　丙 *Bing* **Yang Fire**

Rat

For a Zi (Rat) Month, Ding Fire, Jia Wood and Bing Fire are the Regulating Useful Gods.

Ding Fire and Jia Wood are the preferred or primary Useful Gods for a Geng Metal Day Master born in a Zi (Rat) Month. Meanwhile, Bing Fire, as the secondary Useful God, serves to provide 'warmth' to an otherwise chilly Day Master born in winter.

Without Fire, this Geng Metal Day Master may be afflicted by loneliness in life. Life would be a lackluster.

Rat

Day Master Geng 庚 Metal   **Month** Zi 子 (Rat)

7th day of December – 5th day of January, Gregorian Calendar

In the case of a Geng Metal Day Master born in a Zi (Rat) Month, Metal will invariably tend to be `cold', with Water `chilly'.

Where Water Qi is present in abundance, Metal would consequently be weakened. It would hence be ideal for sufficient Fire to be present to `warm' this Geng Metal Day Master, as well as ensure that Earth is also `warm' and strong enough to keep Water under control.

It is only in the presence of `hot' or `warm' Earth that a Geng Metal Day Master born in a Zi (Rat) Month can expect to survive.

Where Fire is available to penetrate through the Heavenly Stems, only then would Wood be of use as a Useful God.

Only `warm' Wood that also harbors Fire Qi will be able to assist and hence allow Fire to continue `burning' and remain strong, as one of the Useful Gods for this Geng Metal Day Master.

Day Master	Geng 庚 Metal	Month	Zi 子 (Rat)

Commentary

Rat

In addition to the preceding narratives on the potential Structures and scenarios resulting from a Geng Metal Day Master born in a Zi (Rat) Month, the following circumstances also play their respective roles in determining the overall strength of this Day Master's BaZi Chart.

Note:

- Bing Fire and Ding Fire are the preferred or primary Useful God for a Geng Metal Day Master born in a Zi (Rat) Month; with Jia Wood playing the role of a supporting or auxiliary Useful God.

- Gui Water should not penetrate through or be revealed in the Heavenly Stems.

- A Geng Metal Day Master born in a winter month requires Bing Fire to serve as an 'regulator' in 'adjusting' the 'weather' of the BaZi Chart. Then and only then will Ding Fire be able to continue keeping this Geng Metal Day Master 'warm' and well-balanced.

- Jia Wood may be used to produce and ensure the sustainability of Fire Qi in this Geng Metal Day Master's BaZi Chart. Indeed, there could be no better scenario for a Geng Metal Day Master born in a winter month, than to have these Useful Gods present and playing their aforementioned respective roles.

- There is also the need to be mindful of Ren Water and Gui Water, for should they penetrate through the Heavenly Stems, they would be able to weaken and hence undermine the ability of Bing Fire and Ding Fire as Useful Gods for this Geng Metal Day Master.

- Likewise, it would also be highly unfavorable to this chart to have another Geng Metal to be revealed in the Heavenly Stems, since Geng Metal will weaken Jia Wood – which is a Useful God.

- Where Ding Fire and Jia Wood are both revealed – with Bing Fire seen in the Heavenly Stems - this Geng Metal Day Master shall be very successful in life.

- Where Ding Fire and Jia Wood are both revealed – while Bing Fire is missing from the chart - this Geng Metal Day Master shall also be successful in life, although his or her level of success may be limited.

- Where Jia Wood is revealed but Ding Fire is not, this Geng Metal Day Master may only lead an average life, at best.

- Where Bing Fire is revealed and Ding Fire is also found in the Heavenly Stems of the Earthly Branches, this Geng Metal Day Master may enjoy unexpected success in life.

Day Master Geng 庚 Metal		**Month** Zi 子 (Rat)	

Additional Attributes

格局 **Structural Star**	七殺 Seven Killings	偏財 Indirect Wealth	正官 Direct Officer
用神 **Useful God**	Bing 丙 Fire	Jia 甲 Wood	Ding 丁 Fire
Conditions	Where Ding Fire, Jia Wood and Bing Fire are all present, this BaZi Chart is considered superior. Where Ding Fire is present but Jia Wood is missing, this person creates his wealth through his own hands with no help from family. Where Ding Fire and Jia Wood are both revealed – but Bing Fire is not – There's wealth but no noblity.		
Positive Circumstances	Ding Fire and Jia Wood at the Stems while Bing Fire in the Branches		
Negative Circumstances	Where Gui Water (Hurting Officer Star) – penetrates through the Heavenly Stems, this Geng Metal Day Master may lack the drive necessary to succeed in life.		

* Bing Fire and Ding Fire are the most-preferred Useful Gods for a Geng Metal Day Master born in a Zi (Rat) Month.
**Jia Wood serves as the secondary Useful God.

Day Master	Geng 庚 Metal	Month	Zi 子 (Rat)

Summary

- Bing Fire and Ding Fire are the preferred Useful Gods for a Geng Metal Day Master born in a winter month. In the absence of Bing Fire and Ding Fire, this Geng Metal Day Master may be afflicted by povert and or discontentment in life.

- Where Gui Water is revealed in the Heavenly Stems covering the Bing Fire this Geng Metal Day Master having to slog and toil for a living, throughout his or her entire life.

- Where the Earthly Branches forms Water formation – but Ren Water and Gui Water do not penetrate through the Heavenly Stems – with Wu Earth (Indirect Resource Star), this person shall still enjoy reasonable success and good fortune in life; even if Bing Fire and Ding Fire are not revealed.

Geng 庚 Metal Day Master, Born in Twelfth Month 十二月

Chou 丑 (Ox) Month
January 6th - February 3th

Do note that the dates provided above are subject to slight yearly variations. Please refer to your Annual Tong Shu or Joey Yap's Ten Thousand Year Calendar for the accurate dates for each year.

Day Master Geng 庚 Metal   **Month** Chou 丑 (Ox)

日元 Day Master	月 Month
庚 *Geng* **Yang Metal**	丑 *Chou* **Ox** **Yin Earth**

For a Geng Metal Day Master born in a Chou (Ox) Month, a Direct Resource Structure is formed where Ji Earth is revealed as one of the Heavenly Stems.

Where Gui Water is revealed as one of the Heavenly Stems, a Hurting Officer Structure is formed.

Where Xin Metal is revealed as one of the Heavenly Stems, a Goat Blade Structure may be formed when the conditions of the Earthly Branches supports it.

Should, however, neither Ji Earth nor Gui Water happen to be revealed within the Heavenly Stems, one should select the BaZi Chart's most prominent Qi attribute at one's discretion.

| Day Master | Geng 庚 Metal | Month | Chou 丑 (Ox) |

庚金水喜用神提要 Regulating Useful God Reference Guide

月 Month	用神 Useful God
12th Month 十二月 **Yin 寅 (Tiger) Month**	丙 *Bing* **Yang Fire**　丁 *Ding* **Yin Fire**　甲 *Jia* **Yang Wood**

Ox

For a Chou (Ox) Month, Bing Fire, Ding Fire and Jia Wood are the Regulating Useful Gods.

Ding Fire and Jia Wood are the preferred or primary Useful Gods for a Geng Metal Day Master born in a Chou (Ox) Month. Meanwhile, Bing Fire, as the secondary Useful God, serves to provide 'warmth' to an otherwise chilly Day Master born in winter.

Without Fire Qi in this chart, no other Stars can be used as Useful God.

The Qi of Bing Fire and Ding Fire - found in the Earthly Branches of Yin (Tiger), Si (Snake), Wu (Horse), Wei (Goat) and Xu (Dog) – would contain sufficient strength to serve as Useful Gods for this Geng Metal Day Master.

Ox

Day Master Geng 庚 Metal   **Month** Chou 丑 (Ox)

6th day of January – 3rd day of February, Gregorian Calendar

In the case of a Geng Metal Day Master born in a Chou (Ox) Month, the Chou (Ox) Earthly Branch – being one of the Four Graveyards – also serves as storage for excess Metal Qi.

Given the time of the year demarcated by a Chou (Ox) Month, one can only imagine how chilly and freezing the scene may be. The air would be steely and obviously, chilly, while the ground will be invariably covered by snow. The ground is icy.

Under such circumstances, it would be impossible for Earth to produce and strengthen Metal; unless and until Earth is 'warmed' or at least 'heated' to a certain extent by Fire. And Wood would obviously be needed to produce and ensure the continuity of Fire.

Wood and Fire are the indispensable Useful Gods for a Geng Metal Day Master born in a Chou (Ox) Month.

Although a Chou (Ox) Month contains and stores Metal as one of its hidden Qi, Wood however is weak in winter. As such, only 'warm' and dry Wood – which harbors Fire Qi within – would be of use or avail to this Geng Metal Day Master.

Where possible, this Geng Metal Day Master should also avoid encountering additional Water and Metal stars. This is because Water, would surely counter and hence weaken Fire, which is much needed. Consequently, this would only result in the Qi of this Geng Metal Day Master's BaZi Chart becoming colder and colder. And this would also make it much harder for Wood Qi to be produced and thrive, given such a 'chilly' or 'cold' environment.

| Day Master | Geng 庚 Metal | Month | Chou 丑 (Ox) |

Commentary

In addition to the preceding narratives on the potential Structures and scenarios resulting from a Geng Metal Day Master born in a Chou (Ox) Month, the following circumstances also play their respective roles in determining the overall strength of this Day Master's BaZi Chart.

Note:

- Bing Fire, Ding Fire and Jia Wood are the preferred Useful Gods for a Geng Metal Day Master born in a Chou (Ox) Month.

- Ren Water and Gui Water should not penetrate through the Heavenly Stems, as well.

- Where the Earthly Branches form a Metal Structure but Ding Fire is missing from the chart, this Geng Metal Day Master may be afflicted by loneliness in life. (The presence of Bing Fire would be to no avail, since the outcome for this Geng Metal Day Master would still be the same. Certainly, the absence of Ding Fire would only worsen or compound the situation.)

- Where Bing Fire and Ding Fire are both revealed in the Heavenly Stems but Jia Wood is missing from the Four Pillars of Destiny, this Geng Metal Day Master shall be learned and knowledgeable, although he or she may be compelled to slog and toil from scratch, in order to enjoy ultimate success in an entrepreneurial venture in later years of his/her life.

- Where Bing Fire is missing from the Four Pillars of Destiny, this Geng Metal Day Master may only be able to lead a simple, average life at best.

- Where Ji Earth is revealed – which is `wet' or `moist' Earth – it would still be useless as a Resource Star. A Geng Metal Day Master subject to such a circumstance in his or her BaZi Chart would be skillful, although he or she may not be able to capitalize upon such skills to make the most of what life has to offer him or her.

Ox

Day Master Geng 庚 Metal		**Month** Chou 丑 (Ox)	

Additional Attributes

格局 **Structural Star**	七殺 Seven Killings	偏財 Indirect Wealth	正官 Direct Officer
用神 **Useful God**	Bing 丙 Fire	Jia 甲 Wood	Ding 丁 Fire
Conditions	Where Ding Fire, Jia Wood and Bing Fire are all present, this BaZi Chart is considered superior. Where Ding Fire is present but Jia Wood is missing, this person may be extremely talented but do not meet enough opportunities to make use of those talent in his / life. Where Ding Fire and Jia Wood are both revealed – but Bing Fire is not present in the chart, the person has certain character problems that prevent him/her to succeed. Without Bing Fire, there is always a feeling of discontentment.		
Positive Circumstances	Bing Fire and Jia Wood at the Stems while Ding Fire in the Branches		
Negative Circumstances	Where Ren and Gui Water (Output Stars)– penetrates through the Heavenly Stems, this Geng Metal Day Master may lack the drive necessary to succeed in life.		

* *Bing Fire and Ding Fire are the most-preferred Useful Gods for a Geng Metal Day Master born in a Zi (Rat) Month.*

** *Jia Wood serves as the secondary Useful God.*

Day Master	Geng 庚 Metal		Month	Chou 丑 (Ox)

Summary

- Bing Fire and Ding Fire are the preferred Useful Gods for a Geng Metal Day Master born in a winter month. In the absence of Bing Fire and Ding Fire, this Geng Metal Day Master may be afflicted by poverty and or discontentment in life.

- In a Chou month, Bing Fire should appear in the Heavenly Stems, while Ding Fire in the Earthly Branches.

- Jia Wood helps keep the Ji Earth in control. Yi Wood is secondary.

- Where Gui Water is revealed in the Heavenly Stems covering the Bing Fire this Geng Metal Day Master having to slog and toil for a living, throughout his or her entire life.

- Where the Earthly Branches forms Water formation – but Ren Water and Gui Water do not penetrate through the Heavenly Stems – with Ji Earth (Direct Resource Star), this person may still enjoy reasonable success in career but constantly plaque by health problems.

十二月 Twelfth Month

Ox

97

Xin (辛) Metal Day Master

Overview:

Xin 辛 Metal is Yin Metal. It represents jewelry and hence fine or 'polished' Metal. Earth is therefore preferred, in order to produce and strengthen Xin Metal. Ren Water would also be favorable, due to its ability to 'cleanse' Xin Metal and allow the latter to shine. Being 'soft' Metal, it would be preferable not for Xin Metal to encounter Wood – especially when present in abundance.

Xin Metal Day Masters are usually attention-getters or grabbers; be it through their looks or their intellect. In other words, they are people who love being in the spotlight and the focal point of everyone – call it the 'life of the party', if you wish – and if they are not, you can easily count on them to make a scene.

Despite their tough, unyielding disposition, bending their ear is not difficult, if one only knows how to go about persuading them. More often than not, the subtle approach usually triumphs over the sledgehammer approach, in getting the attention of a Xin Metal Day Master – since 'face' value is very important to them. Also sentimental by nature, Xin Metal Day Masters also value their relationships and loved ones.

Xin 辛 Metal Day Master, Born in First Month 正月

Yin 寅 (Tiger) Month
February 4th – March 5th

Do note that the dates provided above are subject to slight yearly variations. Please refer to the Ten Thousand Year Calendar for the accurate transition dates for each year.

| Day Master | Xin 辛 Metal | Month | Yin 寅 (Tiger) |

日元 Day Master	月 Month
辛 *Xin* **Yin Metal**	寅 *Yin* **Tiger** **Yang Wood**

For a Xin Metal Day Master born in a Yin (Tiger) Month, a Direct Wealth Structure is formed where Jia Wood is revealed as one of the Heavenly Stems.

Where Bing Fire is revealed as one of the Heavenly Stems, a Direct Officer Structure is formed.

Where Wu Earth is revealed as one of the Heavenly Stems, a Direct Resource Structure is formed.

Should, however, neither Jia Wood nor Bing Fire nor Wu Earth happen to be revealed within the Heavenly Stems, one should select the BaZi Chart's most prominent Qi attribute at one's discretion.

| Day Master | Xin 辛 Metal | | Month | Yin 寅 (Tiger) |

辛金水喜用神提要 **Regulating Useful God Reference Guide**

Tiger

月 **Month**	用神 **Useful God**
1st Month 正月 Yin 寅 **(Tiger) Month**	己 *Ji* **Yin Earth**　　壬 *Ren* **Yang Water**　　庚 *Geng* **Yang Metal**

For a Yin (Tiger) Month, Ji Earth, Ren Water and Geng Metal are its Regulating Useful Gods.

Where this Xin Metal Day Master is weak, Ji Earth should be used as the source or resource to produce and strengthen Xin Metal.

If this Xin Metal Day Master is to prosper and make good in life, however, much will depend on the presence and strength of Ren Water in this BaZi Chart.

As such, Ren Water and Ji Earth should be used as the preferred Useful Gods, while Geng Metal shall come in useful in a supporting role, in order to make this Xin Metal Day Master a well-balanced and sentimental one.

| Day Master | Xin 辛 Metal | Month | Yin 寅 (Tiger) |

4th day of February – 5th day of March, Gregorian Calendar

In this month, the Wood and Fire Qi (Wealth and Officer Stars), plays a dominant role in this Xin Metal Day Master's chart, compared to Earth and Metal.

Naturally, where Wood Qi is strong or prosperous, Metal Qi would be consequently weak or weakened. As such, where a Xin Metal Day Master meets plenty of Wealth Stars in his or her BaZi Chart, it would be safe to say that this Day Master's Self Element would be weakened as a result.

Tiger

Earth should therefore be used to support Metal. Only with the presence of Earth, Jia Wood (Wealth Star) and Fire (Officer Star) – may also be tolerated and hence used to bring balance to this Xin Metal Day Master.

However, it would not be suitable for this Xin Metal Day Master to meet with Water in abundance. This is because Metal Qi would `leak' and hence be weakened, and in turn Wood Qi is further produced or `grown' in abundance. Abundant water contaminates Earth. The Xin Metal will loose its elegance.

A Xin Metal Day Master who also happens to be born in a Chen (Dragon) Hour of a Yin (Tiger) Month would find that Fire, being bright, would also support Earth in abundance. Under such circumstances, it would only be easy for a Fire Formation to take place involving the Earthly Branches of Yin (Tiger) and Wu (Horse).

The best-case scenario in order to support strong and thriving Metal Qi would hence be `wet' or `moistened' Earth.

| Day Master | Xin 辛 Metal | Month | Yin 寅 (Tiger) |

Commentary

正
月
First Month

寅
Tiger

In addition to the preceding narratives on the potential Structures and scenarios resulting from a Xin Metal Day Master born in a Yin (Tiger) Month, the following circumstances also play their respective roles in determining the overall strength of this Day Master's BaZi Chart.

Note:

- Ji Earth and Ren Water are the preferred Useful Gods.

- It would be best that the Earthly Branches do not unwittingly form a Fire Structure.

- Xin Metal is simply no match for the stronger, more robust nature of Geng Metal. Xin Metal, being Yin Metal, can be symbolized or represented by fine metal, such as jewelry, and is therefore more `genteel' and `polished' by nature. Meeting with extreme Fire will only constraint it's beauty.

- Intense Fire should not and cannot be used to temper or weaken Xin Metal; rather, Water would be the perfect choice to `wash' and `moisten' Xin Metal. This is why Ren Water would be a better choice of Useful God, for a Xin Metal Day Master born this month.

- Ji Earth may also be used to produce and hence strengthen Xin Metal. Wu Earth and Geng Metal should preferably not have to be employed as Useful Gods. It would also be preferable for Ji Earth and Ren Water not to be present side-by-side in the BaZi Chart.

- Wood Qi is dominant in a Yin (Tiger) Month. Where Xin Metal lacks the `power' or ability to counter and hence keep Wood under control, only Ji Earth may be suitably used to produce and strengthen Xin Metal.

Tiger

Day Master Xin 辛 Metal　　　　**Month** Yin 寅 (Tiger)

Additional Attributes

格局 Structural Star	偏印 Indirect Resource	傷官 Hurting Officer
用神 Useful God	Ji 己 Earth	Ren 壬 Water
Conditions	Where both Rob Wealth and Friend Stars are present in the BaZi Chart, this Xin Metal Day Master shall prosper in life.	
Positive Circumstances	It would be ideal for Ji Earth – as a Useful God – to be found from one of the Hidden Stems from the Chou (Ox) or Wei (Goat) Earthly Branches.	
Negative Circumstances	Where either Ji Earth or Ren Water happen to be absent from the BaZi Chart, this Xin Metal Day Master may not be able to achieve the level of success or prosperity, according to his or her actual capacity in life.	

格局 Structural Star	正官 Direct Officer	七殺 Seven Killings
用神 Useful God	Bing 丙 Fire	Ding 丁 Fire
Conditions	Where the Earthly Branches form a Fire Structure – without Geng Metal (Rob Wealth Star) being seen penetrating through the Heavenly Stems – this Xin Metal Day Master would only lead an average life, best.	
Positive Circumstances	Geng Metal and Ren Water are both revealed in the BaZi Chart. This would enjoy an easy, happy life.	
Negative Circumstances	This Xin Metal Day Master is not rooted in a similar Hidden Stem. Also, where Fire is found in certain places or positions in the BaZi Chart, condemning the Xin.	

Day Master	Xin 辛 Metal		Month	Yin 寅 (Tiger)

Additional Attributes

Tiger

格局 Structural Star	傷官 Hurting Officer	食神 Eating God
用神 Useful God	Ren 壬 Water	Gui 癸 Water
Conditions	Where there is an abundance of Water Qi contained within the Earthly Branches - and the former is also revealed in the Heavenly Stems, with Bing Fire (Direct Officer Star) absent – this Xin Metal Day Master may have to struggle a bit during his or her younger years. Olders year would be fine.	
Positive Circumstances	Bing Fire, as a Direct Office Star, penetrates through the Heavenly Stems.	
Negative Circumstances	Bing Fire born at night or covered by Gui Water.	

* Ji Earth and Ren Water are the preferred Useful Gods.

** Jia Wood should be prevented from penetrating through the Heavenly Stems.

| **Day Master** | Xin 辛 Metal | | **Month** | Yin 寅 (Tiger) |

Summary

- Jia Wood and Yi Wood form Wealth Structures with a Xin Metal Day Master born in a Yin (Tiger) Month. Such structures would, however, not only be useless; but also, this Xin Metal Day Master shall not gain or prosper in life, in their presence.

- It would be preferable for a Direct Officer Star to be seen.

- Where the Earthly Branches form a Fire Sormation (Seven Killings Structure), it would be precarious or unfavorable to this Xin Metal Day Master. Where Geng Metal and Ren Water are revealed in the Chart, this person would at least be able to enjoy a smooth-sailing life. With the supportive Luck Pillars, he can still achieve prosperity. The most important element would be Ren Water.

Xin 辛 Metal Day Master, Born in Second Month 二月

Mao 卯 (Rabbit) Month
March 6th – April 4th

Do note that the dates provided above are subject to slight yearly variations. Please refer to the Ten Thousand Year Calendar for the accurate transition dates for each year.

Day Master	Xin 辛 Metal

Month	Mao 卯 (Rabbit)

日元 **Day Master**	月 **Month**

Xin
Yin Metal

Mao
Rabbit
Yin Wood

Rabbit

For a Xin Metal Day Master born in a Mao (Rabbit) Month, an Indirect Wealth Structure is formed where Yi Wood is revealed or not revealed as one of the Heavenly Stems.

| Day Master | Xin 辛 Metal | Month | Mao 卯 (Rabbit) |

辛金水喜用神提要 **Regulating Useful God Reference Guide**

月 Month	用神 Useful God	
2nd Month 二月 Mao 卯 (Rabbit) Month	壬 *Ren* **Yang Water**	甲 *Jia* **Yang Wood**

Rabbit

For a Mao (Rabbit) Month, Ji Earth, Ren Water and Jia Wood are its Regulating Useful Gods.

Where this Xin Metal Day Master is weak, Ji Earth should be used as the source or resource to produce and hence further strengthen Xin Metal.

If this Xin Metal Day Master is to prosper and make good in life, however, much will depend on the presence and strength of Ren Water in this Day Master's BaZi Chart. Ren brings out the best in Xin Metal.

As such, Ren Water and Ji Earth should be used as the preferred Useful Gods, while Geng Metal shall come in useful in a supporting role, in order to make this Xin Metal Day Master a well-balanced and sentimental one.

| **Day Master** Xin 辛 Metal | **Month** Mao 卯 (Rabbit) |

6th day of March – 4th day of April, Gregorian Calendar

Since a Mao (Rabbit) Month denotes one of the spring season months, Wood Qi is at its peak or most prosperous in spring. Xin Metal would, however, be weak.

As such, Earth and Metal are the best Useful Gods for a Xin Metal Day Master born in a Mao (Rabbit) Month.

Since Wood Qi is prosperous in spring, it would invariably counter and control Earth Qi. This means the Xin Metal Day Master's Resource Stars would be controlled and hence weakened.

It would hence be best for this Xin Metal Day Master to avoid encountering additional Wood and Water, in his or her BaZi Chart. This is because both these elements have the capacity to `hurt' and weaken Earth, as well as Metal.

Rabbit

| Day Master | Xin 辛 Metal | Month | Mao 卯 (Rabbit) |

Commentary

In addition to the preceding narratives on the potential Structures and scenarios resulting from a Xin Metal Day Master born in a Mao (Rabbit) Month, the following circumstances also play their respective roles in determining the overall strength of this Day Master's BaZi Chart.

Note:

- It would be favorable to this Xin Metal Day Master, for both Ren Water and Jia Wood to be revealed in the BaZi Chart.

- Where possible, this Xin Metal Day Master should avoid meeting Wu Earth and Ji Earth together. Too much earth buries the Metal

- Where Fire and Earth are revealed in the chart with respective roots in branches of the BaZi Chart, two Ren Water elements would be needed to penetrate through the Heavenly Stems, in order for any structure formed to be a good or at least above-average one.

- Ren Water (Hurting Officer Star) - and Jia Wood (Direct Wealth Star) – are the best choices to complement this Xin Metal Day Master. The absence of either or both would only make for an average BaZi Chart for this Xin Metal Day Master.

- Abundant presence of Earth is truly undesirable. There will be a life full of procrastination and obstacles.

- Roots of Xin Metal in You (Rooster) directly next to the month branch can spell misfortunate at middle age.

二月 Second Month

Rabbit

Rabbit

Day Master Xin 辛 Metal		**Month** Mao 卯 (Rabbit)

Additional Attributes

格局 **Structural Star**	傷官 Hurting Officer	正財 Direct Wealth
用神 **Useful God**	Ren 壬 Water	Jia 甲 Wood
Conditions	Where Ren Water is revealed in the BaZi Chart, this Xin Metal Day Master would be a enjoy a prosperous life.	
Positive Circumstances	Ren Water and Jia Wood in the Heavenly Stems	
Negative Circumstances	In the absence of Jia Wood penetrating through the Heavenly Stems, one instead sees Wu Earth as a Direct Resource Star penetrating through the Heavenly Stems.	

格局 **Structural Star**	傷官 Hurting Officer
用神 **Useful God**	Ren 壬 Water
Conditions	Where Ren Water by itself forms a dominant Hurting Officer Star with this Xin Metal Day Master – and the Earthly Branches form Metal and Water formations – a life full of problems and incessent worries awaits.
Positive Circumstances	Presence of Wu Earth to keep the water at bay
Negative Circumstances	Appearance of Gui Water in the Heavenly Stems

114

Day Master	Xin 辛 Metal	Month	Mao 卯 (Rabbit)

Additional Attributes

格局 **Structural Star**	正官 Direct Officer	七殺 Seven Killings
用神 **Useful God**	Bing 丙 Fire	Ding 丁 Fire
Conditions	Where the relevant Earthly Branches form a Fire Frame. This Chart would be a substandard one. Not even the presence of Wu Earth and Ji Earth would help or alleviate the situation.	
Positive Circumstances	Where the Heavenly Stems encounter two or more Ren Water, both must also be revealed in the BaZi Chart, in order for this Xin Metal Day Master's BaZi Chart to be a well-balanced and favourable one.	
Negative Circumstances	Where no Ren Water penetrates through the Heavenly Stems, this Xin Metal Day Master may be susceptible to poor health and illness throughout his or her entire life.	

* *Ren Water is the preferred Useful God.*

** *Wu Earth and Ji Earth should be prevented from penetrating through the Heavenly Stems.*

二月 Second Month

Rabbit

115

二月 Second Month

卯 Rabbit

| Day Master | Xin 辛 Metal | Month | Mao 卯 (Rabbit) |

Summary

- It would be unfavorable or unsuitable for a Xin Metal Day Master born in a Mao (Rabbit) Month to use Wealth, Officer or Resource Stars as Useful Gods.

- Where a Direct Officer Star is used, Ren Water (Hurting Officer Star) needs to be positioned strategically. Likewise, where a Direct Wealth Star is used, the Geng Metal Rob Wealth Star needs to be positioned strategically.

- Wu Earth or Ji Earth should best be avoided, since both form excessive Resource Stars that would bury this Xin Metal Day Master.

- Excessive Earth means a lackluster life for this Xin Metal Day Master.

Xin 辛 Metal Day Master, Born in Third Month 三月

Chen 辰 (Dragon) Month
April 5th - May 5th

Do note that the dates provided above are subject to slight yearly variations. Please refer to the Ten Thousand Year Calendar for the accurate transition dates for each year.

Day Master Xin 辛 Metal

Month Chen 辰 (Dragon)

日元 **Day Master**	月 **Month**

Xin
Yin Metal

Chen
Dragon
Yang Earth

Dragon

For a Xin Metal Day Master born in a Chen (Dragon) Month, a Direct Resource Structure is formed where Wu Earth is revealed as one of the Heavenly Stems.

Where Yi Wood is revealed as one of the Heavenly Stems, an Indirect Wealth Structure is formed.

Where Gui Water is revealed as one of the Heavenly Stems, an Eating God Structure is formed.

Should, however, neither Wu Earth nor Yi Wood nor Gui Water happen to be revealed within the Heavenly Stems, one should select a Structure according to the BaZi Chart's most prominent Qi attribute at one's discretion.

| Day Master | Xin 辛 Metal | Month | Chen 辰 (Dragon) |

辛金水喜用神提要 **Regulating Useful God Reference Guide**

月 **Month**	用神 **Useful God**
3rd Month 三月 Chen 辰 **(Dragon) Month**	壬 *Ren* **Yang Water** 　 甲 *Jia* **Yang Wood**

Dragon

For a Chen (Dragon) Month, Ren Water and Jia Wood are its most important Regulating Useful Gods.

Where Bing Fire is seen combining with Xin Metal to form Water, Gui Water would be needed to exert at least some control over Bing Fire.

This Xin Metal Day Master would be a prosperous and prominent one, where the Earthly Branches of Hai (Pig), Zi (Rat) and Shen (Monkey) are all present in his or her BaZi Chart.

Xin Metal flourishes with water.

| **Day Master** | Xin 辛 Metal | | **Month** | Chen 辰 (Dragon) |

5th day of April – 5th day of May, Gregorian Calendar

Dragon

A Xin Metal Day Master born in a Chen (Dragon) Month – contains the Hidden Stems of Wu Earth, Yi Wood and Gui Water. Earth Qi features prominently in a Chen (Dragon) Month. As such, where moist Earth supports Xin Metal, while the Water Qi simultaneously graces the Wood, this Xin Metal Day Master would prosper in life.

It would be preferable to use Water and Wood to bring balance to this Xin Metal Day Master's BaZi Chart; instead of Wood and Fire stars. Where possible, Fire should be avoided, since it dries and possibly produce more of the Earth, which is already abundant in a Chen (Dragon) Month. Earth that is too `thick' or hard would only `bury' and `suffocate' Xin Metal.

A Xin Metal Day Master born in a Chen (Dragon) Month should avoid meeting additional Earth, as much as possible.

Day Master	Xin 辛 Metal	Month	Chen 辰 (Dragon)

三月

Third Month

Commentary

In addition to the preceding narratives on the potential Structures and scenarios resulting from a Xin Metal Day Master born in a Chen (Dragon) Month, the following circumstances also play their respective roles in determining the overall strength of this Day Master's BaZi Chart.

Dragon

Note:

- Ren Water and Jia Wood should, preferably, be revealed in the BaZi Chart.

- Wu Earth and Ji Earth should be avoided, if possible. Otherwise Xin Metal would be buried.

- Should all Four Graveyard Earthly Branches of Chen (Dragon), Xu (Dog), Chou (Ox) and Wei (Goat) happen to be present – with no Jia Wood to penetrate to the Heavenly Stems – the overall condition of this Chart would merely be a substandard one. A life full of procrastinations and complaints await.

- Where the Earthly Branches reveal an abundance of Fire Qi, Ren Water would be the utmost choice and priority. And it needs to penetrate through the Heavenly Stems to be effective.

- Where the Earthly Branches form Metal and Water Frames, there is a possibility that this Xin Metal Day Master may be afflicted with poor health and illness throughout his or her life.

| Day Master | Xin 辛 Metal | | Month | Chen 辰 (Dragon) |

Additional Attributes

三月 Third Month

辰 Dragon

格局 Structural Star	傷官 Hurting Officer	正財 Direct Wealth
用神 Useful God	Ren 壬 Water	Jia 甲 Wood
Conditions	A Bing Fire that does not combine away the Xin Metal shall bring prosperity, fame and contentment.	
Positive Circumstances	A bright Bing Fire supporting the Chart. Appearance of Wu Earth and Ji Earth in the Heavenly Stems	
Negative Circumstances	Appearance of Wu Earth and Ji Earth in the Heavenly Stems. Ji Earth next to the Jia Wood.	

格局 Structural Star	正印 Direct Resource	偏印 Indirect Resource
用神 Useful God	Wu 戊 Earth	Ji 己 Earth
Conditions	Where there is an abundance of the Chen (Dragon), Xu (Dog), Chou (Ox) and Wei (Goat) Earthly Branches in the BaZi Chart – which also inadvertently form Resource Formations – and without Jia Wood to penetrate through the Heavenly Stems, this Xin Metal Day Master may possess an obstinate and difficult personality. The abundance of Earth would render this Xin Metal totally useless. This person would encounter lifelong obstructions and chronic illness.	
Positive Circumstances	Jia Wood, as a Direct Wealth Star, penetrates through the Heavenly Stems.	
Negative Circumstances	Appearance of Wu Earth in the Heavenly Stems. Presence of Gui Water to contaminate the Earth.	

Day Master Xin 辛 Metal		**Month** Chen 辰 (Dragon)
	Additional Attributes	

格局 **Structural Star**	正官 Direct Officer	七殺 Seven Killings
用神 **Useful God**	Bing 丙 Fire	Ding 丁 Fire
Conditions	Where the Earthly Branches forms the Fire Frame (Seven Killings Structure) - coupled with the absence of Ren Water penetrating through the Heavenly Stems – this Xin Metal Day Master may find life an uphill struggle.	
Positive Circumstances	Ren Water, as a Hurting Officer Star, penetrates through the Heavenly Stems.	
Negative Circumstances	More than two Bing Fire exist in the Chart.	

Dragon

* *Ren Water is the most-preferred Useful God for a Xin Metal Day Master born in a Chen (Dragon) Month.*

** *Bing Fire should be prevented from penetrating through the Heavenly Stems, and combining with this Xin Metal Day Master, since both Bing Fire and Xin Metal combine to form Water.*

三
月

Third Month

Dragon

| Day Master | Xin 辛 Metal | | Month | Chen 辰 (Dragon) |

Summary

- A Xin Metal Day Master born in a Chen (Dragon) Month should, first and foremost, avoid direct contact with Bing Fire (Direct Officer Star) - in the Heavenly Stems, since both Bing Fire and Xin Metal combine to form Water.

- Where the Earthly Branches meets with additional Water (Eating God or Hurting Officer), this Day Master's Wealth Stars would serve as the most-preferred Useful Gods.

- Where neither Ren Water nor Jia Wood happens to be revealed within the Heavenly Stems of the chart, this Xin Metal Day Master would only lead an average life, at best.

- Where Ren Water does not happen to be revealed in the Heavenly Stems, Gui Water may be used as a substitute or alternative.

- Where there is an abundance of Friend and Rob Wealth Stars in the BaZi Chart, this Xin Metal Day Master may not be blessed with longevity in life.

- Where the appearance of the Wu Earth and Ji Earth in the Heavenly Stems, the chart is sub-par.

Xin 辛 Metal Day Master, Born in Fourth Month 四月

Si 巳 (Snake) Month
May 6th - June 5th

Do note that the dates provided above are subject to slight yearly variations. Please refer to the Ten Thousand Year Calendar for the accurate transition dates for each year.

| Day Master | Xin 辛 Metal | Month | Si 巳 (Snake) |

| 日元 **Day Master** | 月 **Month** |

辛
Xin
Yin Metal

巳
Si
Snake
Yin Fire

Snake

For a Xin Metal Day Master born in a Si (Snake) Month, a Direct Officer Structure is formed where Bing Fire is revealed as one of the Heavenly Stems.

Where Wu Earth is revealed as one of the Heavenly Stems, a Direct Resource Structure is formed.

Should, however, neither Bing Fire nor Wu Earth happen to be revealed within the Heavenly Stems, one should select a Structure according to the BaZi Chart's most prominent Qi attribute at one's discretion.

| Day Master | Xin 辛 Metal | | Month | Si 巳 (Snake) |

辛金水喜用神提要 **Regulating Useful God Reference Guide**

Snake

月 **Month**	用神 **Useful God**
4th Month 四月 **Si** 巳 **(Snake) Month**	壬 *Ren* **Yang Water**　　甲 *Jia* **Yang Wood**　　癸 *Gui* **Yin Water**

For a Si (Snake) Month, Ren Water, Jia Wood and Gui Water are the Regulating Useful Gods.

In addition to its 'cleansing' capabilities, Ren Water's ability to 'adjust' or 'acclimatize' the 'climate' or conditions this Xin Metal Day Master is subject to makes it a prominent Useful God. Coupled with the presence of Jia Wood to control Wu Earth, one can only picture or imagine how 'clear' or 'pristine' the conditions surrounding this Xin Metal Day Master are.

| Day Master | Xin 辛 Metal | Month | Si 巳 (Snake) |

6th day of May – 5th day of June, Gregorian Calendar

Snake

The Si (Snake) Earthly Branch contains the Hidden Stems of Geng Metal, as well as Bing Fire and Wu Earth.

Fire is obviously dominant in a summer month such as a Si (Snake) Month. Consequently, Xin Metal would fall under the control of Fire.

As such, Water would first be needed to `moisten' a Xin Metal Day Master born in a Si (Snake) Month. The Metal element hidden inside the Si (Snake) Earthly Branch may also be employed as a Useful God, under such circumstances.

The best-case scenario would be where there is Metal to support and further strengthen this Xin Metal Day Master. As another alternative, Water may also be used in tandem with Wood to bring balance to this Xin Metal Day Master.

Water and Fire can also be used to make this Xin Metal Day Master a prosperous one.

Metal and Water are the primary Useful Gods for a Xin Metal Day Master born in a Si (Snake) Month. Wood Qi, in small, controlled quantities, may also serve as an auxiliary Useful God. This is because an excess of Wood Qi would invariably produce and bring about a surplus of Fire Qi, which in turn, would exert an overly strong control over Metal and hence this Xin Metal Day Master.

Day Master	Xin 辛 Metal		Month	Si 巳 (Snake)

Commentary

In addition to the preceding narratives on the potential Structures and scenarios resulting from a Xin Metal Day Master born in a Si (Snake) Month, the following circumstances also play their respective roles in determining the overall strength of this Day Master's BaZi Chart.

Snake

Note:

- Ren Water and Gui Water are the preferred Useful Gods.

- A Xin Metal Day Master born in a Si (Snake) Month should avoid meeting Bing Fire, Wu Earth and Ji Earth at the Heavenly Stems, where possible.

- Where Gui Water is revealed but Ren Water remains hidden in the Hidden Stems, this Xin Metal Day Master may prosper and become wealthy in life, although he or she may lack real authority or status as well.

- Where Ren Water and Gui Water are absent or missing from the Heavenly Stems, this Xin Metal Day Master may only lead an average life, at best.

- Where Wu Earth and Bing Fire are present in the Heavenly Stems, this Xin Metal Day Master may suffer from loneliness in life.

- Where the Earthly Branches form a Wood or Fire Frame, this Xin Metal Day Master may only lead an average life, at best.

- Where the Earthly Branches form a Metal Frame – and with Ren Water revealed – this Xin Metal Day Master shall enjoy good and successful outcomes in his or her life's endeavors.

| **Day Master** Xin 辛 Metal | | **Month** Si 巳 (Snake) |

Additional Attributes

Snake

格局 **Structural Star**	正財 Direct Wealth	偏財 Indirect Wealth
用神 **Useful God**	Jia 甲 Wood	Yi 乙 Wood
Conditions	Where the Earthly Branches consist of mainly Wood – (which are Wealth Stars to this Xin Metal Day Master) – along with the presence of Friend and Rob Wealth Stars revealed in the BaZi Chart, this person shall enjoy a life full of abundance and luxuries.	
Positive Circumstances	Geng Metal also appearing in the Heavenly Stems.	
Negative Circumstances	Where Friend and Rob Wealth Stars do not happen to be revealed in the BaZi Chart, the latter's overall structure would tend to be a substandard one.	

| Day Master | Xin 辛 Metal | Month | Si 巳 (Snake) |

Additional Attributes

格局 **Structural Star**	正官 Direct Officer	七殺 Seven Killings
用神 **Useful God**	Bing 丙 Fire	Ding 丁 Fire
Conditions	Where the Earthly Branches forms the Fire Frame – (Seven Killings Structure) – and Ren Water and Gui Water also happen to be revealed in the Chart, this person will enjoy a life of great status, power and authority.	
Positive Circumstances	Ren Water appearing in the Heavenly Stem.	
Negative Circumstances	Where Ren Water and Gui Water do not happen to be revealed in the Heavenly Stems, this Xin Metal Day Master's BaZi Chart would tend to have an overall substandard structure.	

Snake

* *Geng Metal and Xin Metal are the preferred Useful Gods.*

***Bing Fire should be avoided or prevented from penetrating through to the Heavenly Stems.*

| Day Master | Xin 辛 Metal | | Month | Si 巳 (Snake) |

Summary

- Where Water is missing from the chart, he or she may suffer from poverty at least at some point in his or her life.

- Regardless of what structure may be formed within the BaZi Chart, it would still be preferable to have Geng Metal and Xin Metal as Rob Wealth and Friend Stars, respectively, present.

- It would be preferable for the Earthly Branches to form a Metal Structure, with Water also revealed in the BaZi Chart, in order that this Xin Metal Day Master may prosper in life.

Xin 辛 Metal Day Master, Born in Fifth Month 五月

Wu 午 (Horse) Month
June 6 - July 6th

Do note that the dates provided above are subject to slight yearly variations. Please refer to the Ten Thousand Year Calendar for the accurate transition dates for each year.

Day Master Xin 辛 Metal   **Month** Wu 午 (Horse)

日元 **Day Master**	月 **Month**

Xin
Yin Metal

Wu
Horse
Yang Fire

Horse

For a Xin Metal Day Master born in a Wu (Horse) Month, a Seven Killings Structure is formed where Ding Fire is revealed as one of the Heavenly Stems.

Where Ji Earth is revealed as one of the Heavenly Stems, an Indirect Resource Structure is formed.

Should, however, neither Ding Fire nor Ji Earth happen to be revealed within the Heavenly Stems, one should select a Structure according to the BaZi Chart's most prominent Qi attribute at one's discretion.

Day Master	Xin 辛 Metal	Month	Wu 午 (Horse)

辛金水喜用神提要 **Regulating Useful God Reference Guide**

月 **Month**	用神 **Useful God**
5th Month 五月 **Wu 午 (Horse) Month**	壬 己 癸 *Ren* *Ji* *Gui* **Yang Water** **Yin Earth** **Yin Water**

五月

Fifth Month

Horse

For a Wu (Horse) Month, Ren Water, Ji Earth and Gui Water are the Regulating Useful Gods.

However, Ji Earth by itself would not suffice as a Useful God without Ren Water, since it would then lack the 'moisture' or 'wetness' required to play its role as a Useful God. Likewise, Xin Metal simply cannot do without Ji Earth, since the latter is needed to support the former.

As such, both Ren Water and Ji Earth must be present in the BaZi Chart, if each is to play its respective role as a Useful God.

In the absence of Ren Water, Gui Water may be used as a Useful God in its stead.

| **Day Master** Xin 辛 Metal | **Month** Wu 午 (Horse) |

6th day of June – 6th day of July, Gregorian Calendar

Earth would be inevitably dry in mid-summer. Consequently, `dry' or `parched' Earth would not be able to produce `soft' Metal, i.e. Xin Metal.

Similarly, Water that meets Fire in a Wu (Horse) Month would not be able to counter the latter and hence, be `dried-up'.

`Wet' or `moistened' Earth and Water, which also happen to be rooted in their favorable elements, are the `helpful' Stars for this Xin Metal Day Master.

Horse

This Xin Metal Day Master should not meet additional Wood Qi either. This is because Wood will produce and further strengthen Fire, which is already hot enough in summer. And where Fire is too hot or strong, Xin Metal may simply be `melted away'.

Day Master	Xin 辛 Metal		Month	Wu 午 (Horse)

Commentary

In addition to the preceding narratives on the potential Structures and scenarios resulting from a Xin Metal Day Master born in a Wu (Horse) Month, the following circumstances also play their respective roles in determining the overall strength of this Day Master's BaZi Chart.

Note:

- Ren Water and Ji Earth are the preferred Useful Gods. (Where Ji Earth is mentioned, it should be `wet' or `moistened' Earth.)

- Bing Fire and Wu Earth should be avoided, where possible, as well as any possibility of a Fire Structure being formed.

- A Wu (Horse) Month contains Ji Earth as one of its Hidden Stems and within Ji Earth itself, there is `wet' or `moistened' Earth. As such, Ren Water should be prevented from contaminating Ji Earth.

- Without Ren Water, it would be virtually impossible for Ji Earth to be `moistened' or become `wet'. And without Ji Earth, it would be virtually impossible for Xin Metal to be produced and hence further strengthened.

- Where the relevant Earthly Branches a Fire Structure, Ren Water would be needed to penetrate through the Heavenly Stems. A Xin Metal Day Master born in a summer month should employ Ren Water and Gui Water as Useful Gods, as well as be rooted within the Earthly Branches.

- Dry Earth destroys Xin Metal. Water is the saviour.

五
月
Fifth Month

Horse

137

五月 Fifth Month

Horse

Day Master Xin 辛 Metal		**Month** Wu 午 (Horse)

Additional Attributes

格局 **Structural Star**	傷官 Hurting Officer	食神 Eating God	偏印 Indirect Resource
用神 **Useful God**	Ren 壬 Water	Gui 癸 Water	Ji 己 Earth
Conditions	If this Xin Metal Day Master is to enjoy fame in life, Ren Water, Gui Water and Ji Earth must all be present and used together, as Useful Gods.		
Positive Circumstances	Absence of Fire in the Heavenly Stems. Wood and Water to be present		
Negative Circumstances	Excessive Fire and absence of Water in the Chart. Fire appearing on Heavenly Stems		

Day Master Xin 辛 Metal		Month Wu 午 (Horse)

Additional Attributes

格局 **Structural Star**	正官 Direct Officer	七殺 Seven Killings
用神 **Useful God**	Bing 丙 Fire	Ding 丁 Fire
Conditions	Where the Earthly Branches forms the Fire Frame, both Ren Water and Gui Water must be revealed in the BaZi Chart, in order for this Day Master to be a well-balanced, sentimental one.	
Positive Circumstances	Water appearing in the Heavenly Stems. Water is rooted.	
Negative Circumstances	Water is absent or missing from the Four Pillars of Destiny. Where Wu Earth reveals in the Heavenly Stem and where Water is absent or missing from the Four Pillars of Destiny.	

Horse

*   *Ren Water and Ji Earth are the most-preferred Useful Gods.*

** *The Earthly Branches should not form a Fire Structure in the BaZi Chart.*

| Day Master | Xin 辛 Metal | Month | Wu 午 (Horse) |

Summary

- Where Water is absent from the chart, this Day Master may encounter serious difficulties or challenges, whenever he or she enters a Water Luck Period.

- Where the Earthly Branches forms the Fire frame, which forms a Seven Killings Structure to this Xin Metal Day Master – coupled with the absence of Ren Water penetrating through the Heavenly Stems – even the presence of three Gui Water, which penetrate through the Heavenly Stems, will not suffice to `help' bring balance to this Xin Metal Day Master.

- Where Ren Water is revealed in the BaZi Chart but Ji Earth as a Resource Star is not, this Xin Metal Day Master may only lead an average life, at best.

Xin 辛 Metal Day Master, Born in Sixth Month 六月

Wei 未 (Goat) Month
July 7th - August 7th

Do note that the dates provided above are subject to slight yearly variations. Please refer to the Ten Thousand Year Calendar for the accurate transition dates for each year.

Day Master Xin 辛 Metal

Month Wei 未 (Goat)

日元 **Day Master**	月 **Month**

Xin
Yin Metal

Wei
Goat
Yin Earth

Goat

For a Xin Metal Day Master born in a Wei (Goat) Month, an Indirect Resource Structure is formed where Ji Earth is revealed as one of the Heavenly Stems.

Where Ding Fire is revealed as one of the Heavenly Stems, a Seven Killings Structure is formed.

Where Yi Wood is revealed as one of the Heavenly Stems, an Indirect Wealth Structure is formed.

Should, however, neither Yi Wood nor Ji Earth nor Ding Fire happen to be revealed within the Heavenly Stems, one should select a Structure according to the BaZi Chart's most prominent Qi attribute at one's discretion.

| Day Master | Xin 辛 Metal | Month | Wei 未 (Goat) |

辛金水喜用神提要 Regulating Useful God Reference Guide

Goat

月 Month	用神 Useful God
6th Month 六月 Wei 未 (Goat) Month	壬 *Ren* **Yang Water** 庚 *Geng* **Yang Metal** 甲 *Jia* **Yang Wood**

For a Wei (Goat) Month, Ren Water, Geng Metal and Jia Wood are the Regulating Useful Gods.

Ren Water is the preferred or first-choice Useful God, with Geng Metal serving as an 'intermediary' Useful God.

Wu Earth should also be prevented from penetrating through the Heavenly Stems. To serve this purpose and ensure that this Xin Metal Day Master's BaZi Chart is a well-balanced one, Jia Wood may be used to keep Wu Earth under control.

143

Day Master Xin 辛 Metal   **Month** Wei 未 (Goat)

7th day of July – 7th day of August, Gregorian Calendar

Goat

Fire and Earth Qi are very strong in a Wei (Goat) Month. In addition, the Wei (Goat) Earthly Branch – being one of the Four Storages – also serves as storage for excess Wood Qi.

Earth would inevitably be `leaden' and `parched'. As such, Water as a Useful God should first be used to `moisten' Earth, with Metal playing a supporting role in producing Water. Then, and only then, will this Xin Metal Day Master be able to prosper in life.

Wood Stars should be used sparingly especially where Fire Qi is particularly strong. Unless it is wet Wood. This is simply because an abundance of Wood Qi would only produce and lead to an abundance of Fire Qi. Consequently, Fire would exert an overly strong and hence unfavorable control over this Xin Metal Day Master.

Day Master	Xin 辛 Metal		Month	Wei 未 (Goat)

Commentary

In addition to the preceding narratives on the potential Structures and scenarios resulting from a Xin Metal Day Master born in a Wei (Goat) Month, the following circumstances also play their respective roles in determining the overall strength of this Day Master's BaZi Chart.

Note:

Goat

- More attention should be paid towards using Ren Water as a Useful God, with Geng Metal serving as an `intermediary' Useful God.

- Where possible, Ding Fire and Ji Earth should not be revealed in the Heavenly Stems.

- Where both Ren Water and Geng Metal are revealed in the BaZi Chart, this Xin Metal Day Master shall enjoy immense success in life.

- Ji Earth is featured prominently in a Wei (Goat) Month. Consequently, Metal that is `dirtied by' and `buried' under too much Earth would still be what it is: `Contaminated' and `buried' Metal, which would not have the chance to `shine'.

- Should Ding Fire and Ji Earth penetrate through the Heavenly Stems, this Xin Metal Day Master may lack a sense of purpose in life.

六月 Sixth Month

Goat

| **Day Master** Xin 辛 Metal | **Month** Wei 未 (Goat) |

Additional Attributes

格局 **Structural Star**	傷官 Hurting Officer	劫財 Rob Wealth
用神 **Useful God**	Ren 壬 Water	Geng 庚 Metal
Conditions	Provided Wu Earth and Ji Earth – as Resource Stars – do not penetrate through the Heavenly Stems, this Xin Metal Day Master shall enjoy a successful professional or career life.	
Positive Circumstances	Where Wu Earth penetrates through the Heavenly Stems, Jia Wood should also penetrate through the Heavenly Stems, in order to keep Wu Earth under control.	
Negative Circumstances	Ji Earth penetrates to the Heavenly Stems Yi Wood penetrated to the Heavenly Stem and sits next to Geng Metal	

Day Master	Xin 辛 Metal	Month	Wei 未 (Goat)

Additional Attributes

Goat

格局 **Structural Star**	正財 Direct Wealth
用神 **Useful God**	Jia 甲 Wood
Conditions	Where only Wealth Structures are formed, Ren Water and Geng Metal would still be needed, together, as Useful Gods to bring balance to this Xin Metal Day Master's BaZi Chart.
Positive Circumstances	Geng Metal should, preferably, penetrate through the Heavenly Stems.
Negative Circumstances	This Xin Metal Day Master may find it difficult to succeed and prosper in life, should Geng Metal happen to be absent from his or her BaZi Chart.

* Ren Water and Geng Metal are the most-preferred Useful Gods.

147

| **Day Master** | Xin 辛 Metal | **Month** | Wei 未 (Goat) |

Summary

Goat

- A Xin Metal Day Master born in a Wei (Goat) Month is subject to the same principles and conditions governing Xin Metal Day Master born in other summer months. Where Ren Water does not penetrate through the Heavenly Stems, it would obviously be impossible for any good or above-average structures to be formed in this Xin Metal Day Master's BaZi Chart.

- There would be no need to avoid or prevent any Rob Wealth Stars from penetrating through the Heavenly Stems, if a Wealth Structure is to be formed with this Xin Metal Day Master.

- Ren Water present is must desirable. At minimal it would be on above average life.

Xin 辛 Metal Day Master, Born in Seventh Month 七月

Shen 申 (Monkey) Month
August 8th - September 7th

Do note that the dates provided above are subject to slight yearly variations. Please refer to the Ten Thousand Year Calendar for the accurate transition dates for each year.

Day Master Xin 辛 Metal   **Month** Shen 申 (Monkey)

日元 Day Master	月 Month

Xin
Yin Metal

Shen
Monkey
Yang Metal

Monkey

Where the Geng Metal appears on the Heavenly Stem, a Goat Blade Structure may be formed.

For a Xin Metal Day Master born in a Shen (Monkey) Month, a Hurting Officer Structure is formed where Ren Water is revealed as one of the Heavenly Stems.

Where Wu Earth is revealed as one of the Heavenly Stems, a Direct Resource Structure is formed.

Should, however, neither Geng Metal, Ren Water nor Wu Earth happen to be revealed amongst the Heavenly Stems, one should select a Structure according to the BaZi Chart's most prominent Qi attribute at one's discretion.

Day Master	Xin 辛 Metal	Month	Shen 申 (Monkey)

辛金水喜用神提要 Regulating Useful God Reference Guide

月 Month	用神 Useful God

7th Month 七月 Shen 申 (Monkey) Month	壬 *Ren* **Yang Water**	甲 *Jia* **Yang Wood**	戊 *Wu* **Yang Earth**

Monkey

For a Shen (Monkey) Month, Ren Water, Jia Wood and Wu Earth are the Regulating Useful Gods.

Ren Water is the first-choice Useful God, while Jia Wood and Wu Earth are the supporting Useful Gods.

Gui Water, however, may not be appropriately used as a Useful God

Day Master	Xin 辛 Metal	Month	Shen 申 (Monkey)

8th day of August – 7th day of September, Gregorian Calendar

Metal and Water Qi is dominant in a Shen (Monkey) Month. This is because Metal Qi is at its peak or strongest, in autumn.

Where Wood serves as the primary Useful God - with Water to produce and further strengthen Wood - this Xin Metal Day Master shall possess an intelligent personality, with prosperity and wealth to match his or her intelligence.

Wood, Water and Fire stars may also be selected as the Useful Gods for a Xin Metal Day Master born in a Shen (Monkey) Month. Where all three are present in the BaZi Chart, this Xin Metal Day Master shall enjoy fame, authority and fortune in life.

Monkey

Day Master	Xin 辛 Metal	Month	Shen 申 (Monkey)

Commentary

In addition to the preceding narratives on the potential Structures and scenarios resulting from a Xin Metal Day Master born in a Shen (Monkey) Month, the following circumstances also play their respective roles in determining the overall strength of this Day Master's BaZi Chart.

Monkey

Note:

- Geng Metal should, preferably, be revealed as well as penetrate through the Heavenly Stems, in This can form a powerful Goat Blade Structure.

- Where possible, Wu Earth should be avoided or at least, prevented from penetrating through to the Heavenly Stems.

- Where Wu Earth is revealed or present in the Heavenly Stems, this Xin Metal Day Master would only lead an average life, at best. This is because Earth buries Metal.

- Where Geng Metal penetrates through the Heavenly Stems, Ren Water would be needed to weaken and prevent Geng Metal from becoming overly strong.

- Ding Fire can also be selected, in the absence of Ren Water, as the Useful God to forge Geng Metal. This would be a Noble Structure.

- It would only be feasible or acceptable for Wu Earth to be present in the Heavenly Stems, in the presence of a Water Structure, which also penetrates through the Heavenly Stems.

七月
Seventh Month

Monkey

| **Day Master** Xin 辛 Metal | **Month** Shen 申 (Monkey) |

Additional Attributes

格局 **Structural Star**	正印 Direct Resource
用神 **Useful God**	Wu 戊 Earth
Conditions	Where a Direct Resource Star forms its corresponding structure with this Xin Metal Day Master - as well as exerts a control over Ren Water - Jia Wood would be needed to penetrate through the Heavenly Stems if this Xin Metal Day Master is to be a well-balanced one.
Positive Circumstances	Jia Wood appears in the Heavenly Stems.
Negative Circumstances	Jia Wood does not penetrate through the Heavenly Stems.

格局 **Structural Star**	劫財 Rob Wealth
用神 **Useful God**	Geng 庚 Metal
Conditions	Where Geng Metal – as a Rob Wealth Star – penetrates through the Heavenly Stems, it would be unfavourable to this Xin Metal Day Master, where no Ren Water penetrates through the Heavenly Stems as well.
Positive Circumstances	Ren Water appears in the Heavenly Stems.
Negative Circumstances	Absence of Ren Water and Ding Fire.

Day Master	Xin 辛 Metal		Month	Shen 申 (Monkey)

Additional Attributes

格局 **Structural Star**	傷官 Hurting Officer	食神 Eating God
用神 **Useful God**	Ren 壬 Water	Gui 癸 Water
Conditions	Where the Earthly Branches forms Water frame – the absence of Wu Earth as a Resource Star to penetrate through the Heavenly Stems would only allow this Xin Metal Day Master to lead an average life, at best.	
Positive Circumstances	Wu Earth appearing in the Heavenly Stems.	
Negative Circumstances	Where there is an abundance of Water Qi in the Heavenly Stems, it might be difficult for Wu Earth – if present – to serve as a Resource Star. Where Ji Earth appears in the Heavenly Stem and there is an abundance of Water Qi in the Heavenly Stems, it might be difficult for Ji Earth – if present – to serve as a Resource Star.	

Ren Water is the most-preferred Useful God.

七
月

Seventh Month

Monkey

| Day Master | Xin 辛 Metal | | Month | Shen 申 (Monkey) |

Summary

- A Xin Metal Day Master born in a Shen (Monkey) Month is not particularly averse to any type of Useful God.

- The usage of Ren Water as a Useful God should only be done in moderation. Where there is an abundance of Ren Water, Wu Earth may be used to keep Ren Water under control. Likewise, where there is an abundance of Wu Earth, Jia Wood may be used to keep Wu Earth under control.

Monkey

七月 Seventh Month

156

Xin 辛 Metal Day Master, Born in Eighth Month 八月

You 酉 (Rooster) Month
September 8th - October 7th

Do note that the dates provided above are subject to slight yearly variations. Please refer to the Ten Thousand Year Calendar for the accurate transition dates for each year.

| Day Master Xin 辛 Metal | Month You 酉 (Rooster) |

| 日元 Day Master | 月 Month |

辛
Xin
Yin Metal

酉
You
Rooster
Yin Metal

For a Xin Metal Day Master born in a You (Rooster) Month, the Earthly Branch of You (Rooster) is Xin Metal's `Prosperous' position. This unique relationship is not found or contained within any Direct Structures that may be formed in the BaZi Chart.

The Thriving Structure is formed with or without another Xin Metal protruding into the Heavenly Stems.

| Day Master | Xin 辛 Metal | Month | You 酉 (Rooster) |

辛金水喜用神提要 **Regulating Useful God Reference Guide**

月 **Month**	用神 **Useful God**
8th Month 八月 **You 酉 (Rooster) Month**	壬 *Ren* **Yang Water** 甲 *Jia* **Yang Wood**

Rooster

For a You (Rooster) Month, Ren Water and Jia Wood are the Regulating Useful Gods.

Ren Water, as a Useful God, is favored for its `cleansing' capabilities.

Where Wu Earth and Ji Earth are seen in the BaZi Chart, Jia Wood would be needed to keep Earth under control.

Where the relevant Earthly Branches form a Metal Structure, Ding Fire should be used as a substitute for Ren Water, in the latter's absence.

| Day Master | Xin 辛 Metal | | Month | You 酉 (Rooster) |

8th day of August – 7th day of September, Gregorian Calendar

`Prosperous' or Thriving Friends Star features prominently in a You (Rooster) Month.

Since Metal is vibrant in autumn, even strong Wood will be weakened by it. As such, in order to produce and strengthen Wood, which is the Wealth Star of the Day Master, Water can be selected as the Useful God. If both Water and Wood are able to be produced and strengthened simultaneously, this Xin Metal Day Master shall prosper and become wealthy in life.

Where Fire Qi is met, the excessive Metal Qi is kept in control. Where this is seen, the Xin Metal Day Master shall enjoy a high level of status and authority in life.

This Xin Metal Day Master should not meet with additional Metal, since Metal will `jostle' and vie with it for prominence and fights with the Day Master to winning the Wealth Stars (Wood) in the BaZi Chart. Where abundant Metal Qi is seen, the person would not be contented in life.

Where Earth stars are present but Wood absent, Earth would invariably `thicken' and consequently, `bury' Metal in the process.

Day Master	Xin 辛 Metal	Month	You 酉 (Rooster)

Commentary

In addition to the preceding narratives on the potential Structures and scenarios resulting from a Xin Metal Day Master born in a You (Rooster) Month, the following circumstances also play their respective roles in determining the overall strength of this Day Master's BaZi Chart.

Note :

Rooster

- Priority should be given to Ren Water, as a Useful God, in the case of a Xin Metal Day Master born in a You (Rooster) Month.

- Wu Earth and Ji Earth should be avoided or at least prevented from penetrating through the Heavenly Stems.

- Earth should be used in the case where Water is strong.

- Best to avoid encountering Ding Fire in the Heavenly Stems. Otherwise, this Xin Metal Day Master may struggle to achieve success in life.

- Where Ding Fire and Ren Water combine to form Wood – or Bing Fire and Xin Metal combine to form Water – this Xin Metal Day Master may display a tendency towards making quick gains or profits in life, without regard for the long-term consequences of his or her actions. He or she may also lack ambition and the drive needed to produce sustainable success in life.

- Where Xin Metal is present in abundance but Ren Water is missing, this Xin Metal Day Master shall possess an honest, clear conscience and personality.

- Where only Yi Wood – an Indirect Wealth Star – is present in this Xin Metal Day Master's BaZi Chart, he or she may only be able to lead an average life, at best.

- This Xin Metal Day Master may also be predisposed towards heaping the blame on others for his or her failures and shortcomings, without first reflecting inwards. This is because Yi Wood lacks the strength or Qi to `loosen' and hence keep Earth under control. Consequently, its appearance may only be superficial, since Yi Wood would not be able to serve any real purpose at all by its presence.

161

Day Master Xin 辛 Metal　　　　**Month** You 酉 (Rooster)

Additional Attributes

格局 **Structural Star**	傷官 Hurting Officer	正財 Direct Wealth
用神 **Useful God**	Ren 壬 Water	Jia 甲 Wood
Conditions	Where Ren Water (Hurting Officer Star), produces Wood (Wealth Star), this Xin Metal Day Master shall enjoy a successful career or professional life. Where Wu Earth penetrates through the Heavenly Stems, however, this Xin Metal Day Master may encounter more than his or her fair share of failure in life.	
Positive Circumstances	Absence of Ji Earth in the Heavenly Stems. Presence of Bing Fire in the chart. Absence of Ji Earth in the Heavenly Stems.	
Negative Circumstances	Wu Earth, as a Resource Star, penetrates through the Heavenly Stems.	

格局 **Structural Star**	傷官 Hurting Officer	比肩 Friend
用神 **Useful God**	Ren 壬 Water	Xin 辛 Metal
Conditions	Where Metal and Water are present simultaneously, this Xin Metal Day Master shall prosper in life. This is however subject to the condition that the Geng Metal (Rob Wealth Star) is not revealed and does not penetrate through the Heavenly Stems.	
Positive Circumstances	This Xin Metal Day Master would be a strong, thriving one in the absence of Ren Water; provided Ding Fire as a Seven Killings Star is also employed as a Useful God.	
Negative Circumstances	Geng Metal penetrates to the Heavenly Stems. Abundant Earth element appearing on the Heavenly Stems and Earthly Branches.	

| Day Master | Xin 辛 Metal | | Month | You 酉 (Rooster) |

Additional Attributes

格局 **Structural Star**	正印 Direct Resource	偏印 Indirect Resource
用神 **Useful God**	Wu 戊 Earth	Ji 己 Earth
Conditions	Where there is an abundance of Resource Stars in the BaZi Chart, this Xin Metal Day Master may be akin to a defenceless person who does not really possess any 'weapons'.	
Positive Circumstances	Jia Wood present and rooted in the chart to control the Earth. Presence of Jia Wood to combine away the Ji Earth.	
Negative Circumstances	Excessive Wu and Ji Earth appearing on the Heavenly Stems.	

Rooster

* *Ren Water is the most-preferred Useful God.*

**This Xin Metal Day Master should avoid encountering Ji Earth, as well.*

| Day Master | Xin 辛 Metal | | Month | You 酉 (Rooster) |

Summary

- Where only Metal Stars are present in this Xin Metal Day Master's BaZi Chart, Water may be suitably used to weaken and keep excess Metal Qi under control.

- It would be preferable or more favorable to this Xin Metal Day Master for it to meet a Direct Wealth Star with Jia Wood instead of an Indirect Wealth Star with Yi Wood.

- Direct Officer and Seven Killings are secondary choices when it comes to Useful Gods. However, in the absence of good-quality Water, Fire may be selected.

Rooster

Xin 辛 Metal Day Master, Born in Ninth Month 九月

Xu 戌 (Dog) Month
October 8th - November 6th

Do note that the dates provided above are subject to slight yearly variations. Please refer to the Ten Thousand Year Calendar for the accurate transition dates for each year.

| Day Master | Xin 辛 Metal | Month | Xu 戌 (Dog) |

| 日元 **Day Master** | 月 **Month** |

Xin
Yin Metal

Xu
Dog
Yang Earth

Dog

For a Xin Metal Day Master born in a Xu (Dog) Month, a Direct Resource Structure is formed where Wu Earth is revealed as one of the Heavenly Stems.

Where Ding Fire is revealed as one of the Heavenly Stems, a Seven Killings Structure is formed.

Where Xin Metal is revealed as another one of the Heavenly Stems, a Friend Structure may be formed. Should, however, either Ding Fire, Xin Metal, or Wu Earth not happen to be revealed within the Heavenly Stems, one should select a Structure according to the BaZi Chart's most prominent Qi attribute at one's discretion.

| Day Master | Xin 辛 Metal | Month | Xu 戌 (Dog) |

辛金水喜用神提要 Regulating Useful God Reference Guide

戌
Dog

月 Month	用神 Useful God
9th Month 九月 **Xu 戌 (Dog) Month**	壬 *Ren* **Yang Water** 甲 *Jia* **Yang Wood**

For a Xu (Dog) Month, Ren Water and Jia Wood are the Regulating Useful Gods.

In a Xu (Dog) Month, Fire and Earth Qi are considered 'diseased' or unfavorable elements to this Xin Metal Day Master. As such, Water and Wood are the 'Medicating' Useful Gods, in countering the potential problems brought about by negative Fire and Earth.

Ren Water helps cleanse the Xin Metal.

Day Master Xin 辛 Metal   **Month** Xu 戌 (Dog)

8th day of October – 7th day of November, Gregorian Calendar

In the case of a Xin Metal Day Master born in a Xu (Dog) Month, both Fire and Earth can be found in abundance.

Since Earth is invariably `leaden' and `thick' in the autumn. It is therefore advisable to avoid encountering additional Earth and Metal Qi, which serves no purpose in bettering this Day Master. Earth only serves to bury the Metal.

Dog

Water should hence be used as the primary Useful God, in tandem with Wood as the secondary Useful God to weaken this overly strong Xin Metal Day Master to a certain extent.

Wood that is rooted in its resource - Water, would be ideal. This is helps the Xin to be thriving and less `brittle'. If such a scenario is met, this Xin Metal Day Master shall prosper and become wealthy in life.

There should not be an abundance of Fire Qi as well, as Fire does have the propensity to produce and hence further strengthen Earth, which would also be `parched' and leaden.

Day Master	Xin 辛 Metal		Month	Xu 戌 (Dog)

Commentary

In addition to the preceding narratives on the potential Structures and scenarios resulting from a Xin Metal Day Master born in a Xu (Dog) Month, the following circumstances also play their respective roles in determining the overall strength of this Day Master's BaZi Chart.

Note:

- Jia Wood is the preferred or primary Useful God, with Ren Water serving as the secondary Useful God.

- Where possible, Ji Earth should be prevented from penetrating through the Heavenly Stems.

- Where only Wu Earth is revealed in the Heavenly Stems, this Xin Metal Day Master would only lead an average life, at best. Where both Wu Earth and Ji Earth are revealed, this Xin Metal Day Master may lack a sense of purpose or direction in life.

- Where the relevant Earthly Branches form a Water Structure – while both Ren Water and Jia Wood are revealed in the Heavenly Stems – this Xin Metal Day Master shall enjoy a life of quality and prosperity.

- Where Jia Wood happens to be absent in the case of a Xin Metal Day Master born in a Xu (Dog) Month, he or she may struggle to attain success or recognition in life.

九月 Ninth Month

戌 Dog

169

Day Master Xin 辛 Metal   **Month** Xu 戌 (Dog)

Additional Attributes

Dog

格局 **Structural Star**	傷官 Hurting Officer	正財 Direct Wealth
用神 **Useful God**	Ren 壬 Water	Jia 甲 Wood
Conditions	Where Ren Water is revealed – while the Earthly Branches also forms a Water Structure – this Xin Metal Day Master shall succeed in life.	
Positive Circumstances	Absence of Ji Earth means there is no contamination in the Water. Ji Earth is present in the branches.	
Negative Circumstances	Ji Earth revealed in the Heavenly Stems. Ji Earth is next to the Jia Wood.	

格局 **Structural Star**	正官 Direct Officer
用神 **Useful God**	Bing 丙 Fire
Conditions	Where there is a Chen (Dragon) Earthly Branch aligned directly in the Hour Pillar, this Xin Metal Day Master shall prosper in life.
Positive Circumstances	It would be ideal for this Xin Metal Day Master to be born in a Ren Water-Chen (Dragon) Hour.
Negative Circumstances	Ji Earth penetrates to the Stems to bury Metal.

Day Master	Xin 辛 Metal		Month	Xu 戌 (Dog)

Additional Attributes

格局 **Structural Star**	食神 Eating God
用神 **Useful God**	Gui 癸 Water
Conditions	Gui Water, as an Eating God Star, forms its corresponding structure with this Xin Metal Day Master. Although it may even replace Ren Water as a Hurting Officer Star, this Xin Metal Day Master may find it difficult to prosper in life.
Positive Circumstances	Absence of Ji Earth and Bing Fire.
Negative Circumstances	Wu Earth, as a Resource Star, penetrates through the Heavenly Stems.

Dog

Ren Water and Jia Wood are the preferred Useful Gods.

BaZi Structures & Structural Useful Gods 格局與格局用神

| Day Master | Xin 辛 Metal | | Month | Xu 戌 (Dog) |

Summary

- Fire and Earth are considered `diseased' or unfavorable elements to a Xin Metal Day Master born in a Xu (Dog) Month; while Water and Wood are `Medicating' Useful Gods to counter any potential problems brought about by Fire and Earth.

Dog

Xin 辛 Metal Day Master, Born in Tenth Month 十月

Hai 亥 (Pig) Month
November 7th - December 6th

Do note that the dates provided above are subject to slight yearly variations. Please refer to the Ten Thousand Year Calendar for the accurate transition dates for each year.

Day Master Xin 辛 Metal

Month Hai 亥 (Pig)

Pig

日元 Day Master	月 Month

Xin
Yin Metal

Hai
Pig
Yin Water

For a Xin Metal Day Master born in a Hai (Pig) Month, a Hurting Officer Structure is formed where Ren Water is revealed as one of the Heavenly Stems.

Where Jia Wood is revealed as one of the Heavenly Stems, a Direct Wealth Structure is formed.

Should, however, neither Ren Water nor Jia Wood happen to be revealed within the Heavenly Stems, one should select a Structure according to the BaZi Chart's most prominent Qi attribute at one's discretion.

| Day Master | Xin 辛 Metal | Month | Hai 亥 (Pig) |

辛金水喜用神提要 **Regulating Useful God Reference Guide**

月 Month	用神 Useful God
10th Month 十月 Hai 亥 (Pig) Month	壬 *Ren* **Yang Water** 丙 *Bing* **Yang Fire**

亥 Pig

For a Hai (Pig) Month, Ren Water and Bing Fire are the Regulating Useful Gods.

Ren Water is the first-choice or primary Useful God, with Bing Fire serving as the secondary Useful God to this Xin Metal Day Master.

Where possible, `clear' or `pristine' Water should be employed as a Useful God, if this Xin Metal Day Master is to attain fame in life. In any case, both Ren Water and Bing Fire are important as Useful Gods, for both do play respective roles with regard to this Xin Metal Day Master. Bing Fire brings shine and glitter to the Xin Metal.

十月 Tenth Month

Pig

| Day Master | Xin 辛 Metal | | Month | Hai 亥 (Pig) |

7th day of November – 6th day of December, Gregorian Calendar

The Qi of Xin Metal born in this month would be rather chilly, with Earth Qi extremely weak in winter. Warmth is desperately needed for survival.

The presence of Fire will `warm' the Water, which is obviously cold in winter, while `warm' or `warmed' Earth would then have the capacity to produce Metal. It would be preferable for these Useful Gods to possess the preceding qualities, in creating the ideal scenario or `environment' for a Xin Metal Day Master born in a Hai (Pig) Month.

It must also be noted that without Fire, Earth could not possibly be `warmed' to serve its purpose as a Useful God. Fire is, in fact, indispensable as a Useful God to this Xin Metal Day Master, for its very presence allows the elements of Metal, Earth and Wood to be `warmed' and hence become `useable' as Useful Gods, in turn.

It should hence be evident as to why `warm' or `warmed' Earth would be an ideal choice of Useful God for a Xin Metal Day Master born in a Hai (Pig) Month. This is because such Earth has the dual-capacity of producing and hence further strengthening Metal, while keeping Water under control as well.

Furthermore, Metal may be used to `assist' a Xin Metal Day Master born during an hour whereby Fire or Earth happens to be strong, since this would then enhance this Day Master's wealth luck in life.

Day Master	Xin 辛 Metal	Month	Hai 亥 (Pig)

Commentary

In addition to the preceding narratives on the potential Structures and scenarios resulting from a Xin Metal Day Master born in a Hai (Pig) Month, the following circumstances also play their respective roles in determining the overall strength of this Day Master's BaZi Chart.

Note:

- Ren Water is the first-choice or primary Useful God, while Bing Fire serves as the secondary Useful God. Ren helps Xin to shine while Bing Fire allows it to glitter.

- It would be preferable for this Xin Metal Day Master to avoid encountering Wu Earth in his or her BaZi Chart. Wu Earth buries Xin Metal.

- Where both Ren Water and Bing Fire are simultaneously employed as Useful Gods, they should not be aligned or found side-by-side one another in the BaZi Chart, though. The ocean and the Sun are interconnected.

- The 'environment' of a Xin Metal Day Master born in a Hai (Pig) Month would be inevitably cold, due to the winter season. Since Xin Metal also happens to be 'soft' or 'pliant' by nature, it should be 'shielded' or 'protected' against the chilly air of the winter season.

- Where Bing Fire is not revealed in the Heavenly Stems – but Ren Water is instead revealed - this Xin Metal Day Master shall prosper and become wealthy in life, particularly if he or she possesses entrepreneurial talents.

- Where Jia Wood is present in abundance but Wu Earth happens to be missing from the BaZi Chart, this Xin Metal Day Master will possess an honest personality, regardless of how wealthy he or she becomes in life.

- Where Ren Water and Gui Water form their respective structures with this Xin Metal Day Master – and are also revealed in the Heavenly Stems – this Xin Metal Day Master may display an inclination towards wandering aimlessly, without any particular sense of purpose or direction, in life.

- Where Bing Fire is missing from the Four Pillars of Destiny, this Xin Metal Day Master may only lead an average life, at best. Without Bing Fire, there would be lack of happiness.

Day Master Xin 辛 Metal　　　**Month** Hai 亥 (Pig)

Additional Attributes

亥
Pig

格局 Structural Star	傷官 Hurting Officer	正官 Direct Officer
用神 Useful God	Ren 壬 Water	Bing 丙 Fire
Conditions	Where the Ren Water (Hurting Officer Star), encounters another Officer Star and both are revealed in the Heavenly Stems, this Xin Metal Day Master shall enjoy immense success in his or her career-related pursuits. This is a special condition where both opposing stars can meet harmoniously.	
Positive Circumstances	It is imperative that the Earthly Branches that have Bing Fire as their Heavenly Stems do not encounter and combine with one another.	
Negative Circumstances	Ding Fire next to Ren Water. Another Xin Metal next to the Bing Fire.	

格局 Structural Star	正印 Direct Resource
用神 Useful God	Wu 戊 Earth
Conditions	Where Bing Fire (Direct Officer Star) – is missing from the BaZi Chart, this Xin Metal Day Master shall possess only an artistic or creative flair in life. But may suffer emotional setbacks.
Positive Circumstances	Presence of Ding Fire to support the Earth.
Negative Circumstances	Gui Water next to the Wu Earth.

| Day Master | Xin 辛 Metal | Month | Hai 亥 (Pig) |

Additional Attributes

十月 Tenth Month

Pig

格局 **Structural Star**	傷官 Hurting Officer
用神 **Useful God**	Ren 壬 Water
Conditions	Where only Ren Water is seen in the absence of Bing Fire– it would be preferable not to have Wu Earth penetrating through the Heavenly Stems.
Positive Circumstances	Absence of Wu Earth in the Heavenly Stems.
Negative Circumstances	Wu Earth, as a Direct Resource Star, penetrates through the Heavenly Stems.

* Ren Water and Bing Fire are the preferred Useful Gods.

179

| Day Master | Xin 辛 Metal | | Month | Hai 亥 (Pig) |

亥
Pig

Summary

- Ren Water forms a very powerful Hurting Officer Structure with Xin Metal Day Master born in a Hai (Pig) Month.

- As far as Metal Day Masters are concerned, 'clear' or 'pristine' Ren Water is preferred as a Hurting Officer Star. In addition, Wu and Ji Earth should not be allowed to 'contaminate' Water either.

- Where Bing Fire is missing from the BaZi Chart, this Xin Metal Day Master may struggle in achieve happiness and satisfaction in life.

Xin 辛 Metal Day Master, Born in Eleventh Month 十一月

Zi 子 (Rat) Month
December 7th - January 5th

Do note that the dates provided above are subject to slight yearly variations. Please refer to the Ten Thousand Year Calendar for the accurate transition dates for each year.

Day Master Xin 辛 Metal   **Month** Zi 子 (Rat)

日元 **Day Master**	月 **Month**
 Xin **Yin Metal**	 *Zi* **Rat** **Yang Water**

For a Xin Metal Day Master born in a Zi (Rat) Month, an Eating God Structure is formed regardless if Gui Water is revealed or not as a Heavenly Stem.

| Day Master | Xin 辛 Metal | Month | Zi 子 (Rat) |

辛金水喜用神提要 **Regulating Useful God Reference Guide**

月 Month	用神 Useful God
11th Month 十一月 Zi 子 (Rat) Month	丙 戊 壬 甲 *Bing* *Wu* *Ren* *Jia* **Yang Fire** **Yang Earth** **Yang Water** **Yang Wood**

Rat

For a Zi (Rat) Month, Bing Fire, Wu Earth, Ren Water and Jia Wood are the Regulating Useful Gods.

Bing Fire remains indispensable as a Useful God, since it helps to 'warm' things out and hence thaw the chill brought about by the winter season.

As long as Bing Fire is present in the BaZi Chart, the other Useful Gods may be used interchangeably to ensure that this Xin Metal Day Master remains well-balanced and sentimental.

Day Master Xin 辛 Metal   **Month** Zi 子 (Rat)

7th day of December – 5th day of January, Gregorian Calendar

A Xin Metal Day Master born in a Zi (Rat) Month, Metal will invariably tend to be `cold', with Water `chilly'.

Since Xin Metal is weakened by Water, Fire should be used to `warm' and hence ensure that Xin Metal at least remains well-balanced.

Metal, as a Companion Star to Xin Metal, supports and strengthens the latter, a Xin Metal Day Master born in a Zi (Rat) Month would then be a sentimental and thriving one.

`Hot' or `blazing' Wood that also harbors Fire Qi will assist and allow Fire to continue `burning' and hence remain strong, as one of the Useful Gods for this Xin Metal Day Master.

Although Earth is this Xin Metal Day Master's Resource Star, it does have the capacity to `contaminate' Water. As such, Earth should not be present or used in abundance.

Day Master	Xin 辛 Metal		Month	Zi 子 (Rat)

Commentary

In addition to the preceding narratives on the potential Structures and scenarios resulting from a Xin Metal Day Master born in a Zi (Rat) Month, the following circumstances also play their respective roles in determining the overall strength of this Day Master's BaZi Chart.

Note:

- Bing Fire is the preferred or primary Useful God for a Xin Metal Day Master born in a Zi (Rat) Month.

- Where possible, this Xin Metal Day Master should avoid meeting Gui Water as well.

- For the three winter months of Hai (Pig), Zi (Rat) and Chou (Ox), Bing Fire remains indispensable as a `arbitrator' to `adjust' the `weather' and hence Qi of Xin Metal Day Masters born in any of those months. This is all the more important, since Xin Metal is Yin and hence `soft' or `weaker' Metal.

- If Bing Fire is to play its role as a Useful God, however, it must be rooted in the Earthly Branches. This is because Bing Fire that merely `floats' in the Heavenly Stems lacks the strength to bring actual `warmth' to this Xin Metal Day Master, while Ding Fire simply cannot substitute for Bing Fire.

- The Useful God for a Xin Metal Day Master born in a winter month should be able to serve as an `arbitrator' to `adjust' the `weather' of the BaZi Chart. This is why the absence of Bing Fire would already be a setback to this Xin Metal Day Master. Without Bing Fire, the person would lack happiness or achievements in life.

- Where possible, Gui Water should also be avoided or at least prevented from penetrating through the Heavenly Stems. The presence of Ren Water - hidden within the Earthly Branches – would be harmless to this Xin Metal Day Master.

- Where Bing Fire and Ren Water are both revealed, this Xin Metal Day Master shall be blessed with fame and fortune in life. This is because Bing Fire and Ren Water is interdependent. A good and prosperous life is to be expected.

- Where Ren Water and Wu Earth both penetrate through the Heavenly Stems, this Xin Metal Day Master shall only lead an average life, at best.

- Where the relevant Earthly Branches form a Water Structure - with Ren Water also revealed in the Heavenly Stems but Wu Earth is not – this Xin Metal Day Master may suffer from loneliness, and may even find it difficult to make significant progress in life.

185

十一月

Eleventh Month

Rat

| **Day Master** Xin 辛 Metal | | **Month** Zi 子 (Rat) |

Additional Attributes

格局 **Structural Star**	正官 Direct Officer	傷官 Hurting Officer
用神 **Useful God**	Bing 丙 Fire	Ren 壬 Water
Conditions	Where Wu Earth does not penetrate through the Heavenly Stems, this Xin Metal Day Master shall prosper in life.	
Positive Circumstances	Born before sunset. Presence of Bing Fire in the Branches.	
Negative Circumstances	Wu Earth penetrates through the Heavenly Stems.	

| Day Master | Xin 辛 Metal | Month | Zi 子 (Rat) |

Additional Attributes

Rat

格局 Structural Star	傷官 Hurting Officer
用神 Useful God	Ren 壬 Water
Conditions	The Earthly Branches forming a Water Structure. In the event Bing Fire happen to be missing from the chart, the person may suffer from poverty in life, no matter how learned or knowledgeable he or she may be.
Positive Circumstances	Bing Fire should penetrate through the Heavenly Stems.
Negative Circumstances	Absence of Bing Fire in the chart.

* *Bing Fire and Ding Fire are the preferred Useful Gods.*

** *In a Zi (Rat) Month, Gui Water should be prevented from penetrating through the Heavenly Stems.*

十一月 Eleventh Month

Rat

Day Master Xin 辛 Metal   **Month** Zi 子 (Rat)

Summary

- Where the Earthly Branches encounter a Water Frame in the case of a Xin Metal Day Master born in a Zi (Rat) Month, the Heavenly Stems of Geng Metal and Xin Metal may form a Super Vibrant Water (Run Xia 潤下) Structure. Bing Fire should, however, not be absent or missing from the BaZi Chart, for the preceding scenario to take place. Otherwise, the absence of Bing Fire would only result in any structure being formed becoming a substandard one. Bing Fire necessary to keep this chart alive and the water warm.

- Where a Super Vibrant Water (Run Xia 潤下) Structure is formed, this Xin Metal Day Master should preferably be entering a Wood Luck Period. In any case, he or she should not be entering a Fire Luck Period. Water Luck is secondary.

- Gui Water should be prevented from penetrating through the Heavenly Stems at all costs.

- Where two Xin Metal Heavenly Stems vie to combine with Bing Fire in the BaZi Charts of female Xin Metal Day Masters born in a Zi (Rat) Month, married female Xin Metal Day Masters may sorely lack or miss the company of their husbands, in their conjugal relationships.

- Where Ren Water is present but Bing Fire absent, this Xin Metal Day Master may suffer from loneliness, or even be inclined towards living a solitary, `hermit-like' life. Where Bing Fire is present in abundance but Ren Water is missing, this Xin Metal Day Master shall possess excellent business and financial acumen.

- Without Bing Fire, the person would lack happiness and satisfaction in life.

188

Xin 辛 Metal Day Master, Born in Twelfth Month 十二月

Chou 丑 (Ox) Month
January 6th - February 3th

Do note that the dates provided above are subject to slight yearly variations. Please refer to the Ten Thousand Year Calendar for the accurate transition dates for each year.

| **Day Master** Xin 辛 Metal | **Month** Chou 丑 (Ox) |

| 日元 **Day Master** | 月 **Month** |

Xin
Yin Metal

Chou
Ox
Yin Earth

For a Xin Metal Day Master born in a Chou (Ox) Month, an Indirect Resource Structure is formed where Ji Earth is revealed as one of the Heavenly Stems.

Where Gui Water is revealed as one of the Heavenly Stems, an Eating God Structure is formed.

Should, however, neither Ji Earth nor Gui Water happen to be revealed within the Heavenly Stems, one should select the BaZi Chart's most prominent Qi attribute at one's discretion.

| Day Master | Xin 辛 Metal | Month | Chou 丑 (Ox) |

辛金水喜用神提要 **Regulating Useful God Reference Guide**

月 **Month**	用神 **Useful God**

12th Month 十二月
Yin 寅 (Tiger) Month

丙	壬	戊	己
Bing	*Ren*	*Wu*	*Ji*
Yang Fire	**Yang Water**	**Yang Earth**	**Yin Earth**

Ox

For a Chou (Ox) Month, Bing Fire, Ren Water, Wu Earth and Ji Earth are the Regulating Useful Gods.

In ranking the importance of these Useful Gods, Bing Fire would occupy the topmost position, followed by Ren Water, Wu Earth and Ji Earth in descending order.

Under no circumstances, however, should Bing Fire be missing or lacking in this Xin Metal Day Master's BaZi Chart.

Day Master Xin 辛 Metal   **Month** Chou 丑 (Ox)

6th day of January – 3rd day of February, Gregorian Calendar

Chou (Ox) Earthly Branch – being one of the Four Graveyards – also serves as storage for excess Metal Qi. As such, Xin Metal would be rooted in its source of Metal Qi.

Given the time of the year demarcated by a Chou (Ox) Month, one can imagine how chilly and freezing the scene may be. The sky would be steely and obviously, chilly, while the ground will be invariably covered by snow.

As such, Fire is needed to `warm' this Xin Metal Day Master. Since Wood produces Fire, Wood should not be missing or lacking from this Xin Metal Day Master's BaZi Chart. Wood and Fire are the indispensable Useful Gods for a Xin Metal Day Master born in a Chou (Ox) Month.

Although a Chou (Ox) Month contains and stores Metal as one of its hidden Qi, Wood however is weak in winter. Only `warm' or `blazing' Wood – which harbors Fire Qi within – would be of use or avail to this Xin Metal Day Master.

Where possible, this Xin Metal Day Master should also avoid encountering additional Water and Metal Qi. This is because Water would surely counter and weaken the all important Fire Qi, which is much needed. Consequently, this would only result in the Qi of this Xin Metal Day Master's BaZi Chart becoming colder and colder.

| Day Master | Xin 辛 Metal | | Month | Chou 丑 (Ox) |

Commentary

Ox

In addition to the preceding narratives on the potential Structures and scenarios resulting from a Xin Metal Day Master born in a Chou (Ox) Month, the following circumstances also play their respective roles in determining the overall strength of this Day Master's BaZi Chart.

Note:

- Bing Fire is the most-preferred Useful God for a Xin Metal Day Master born in a Chou (Ox) Month.

- A Xin Metal Day Master born in a Chou (Ox) Month should avoid encountering Gui Water, where possible.

- The Useful Gods for a Xin Metal Day Master born in a Chou (Ox) Month are basically the same as those for a Xin Metal Day Master born in a Zi (Rat) Month. Nevertheless, Bing Fire is all the more important and hence indispensable to a Xin Metal Day Master born in a Chou (Ox) Month, compared to his or her counterpart born in a Zi (Rat) Month.

- Where Bing Fire is revealed in the Heavenly Stems but Ren Water is not, this Xin Metal Day Master shall prosper and become wealthy in life; although he or she may lack fame or authority as well.

- Where Ren Water is revealed in the Heavenly Stems but Bing Fire is not, this Xin Metal Day Master may be afflicted by poverty in life; regardless of how learned or knowledgeable he or she may be.

- Ren Water and Bing Fire are the interdependent stars. One cannot be without the other.

Day Master Xin 辛 Metal   **Month** Chou 丑 (Ox)

Additional Attributes

格局 **Structural Star**	正官 Direct Officer	傷官 Hurting Officer
用神 **Useful God**	Bing 丙 Fire	Ren 壬 Water
Conditions	Where Wu Earth does not penetrate through the Heavenly Stems, this Xin Metal Day Master shall prosper in life.	
Positive Circumstances	Presence of Ren Water to support the light. Absence of Ji Earth.	
Negative Circumstances	Wu Earth, as a Resource Star, penetrates through the Heavenly Stems.	

十二月 Twelfth Month

Ox

194

格局 **Structural Star**	**傷官** Hurting Officer

Day Master	Xin 辛 Metal		Month	Chou 丑 (Ox)

Additional Attributes

格局 **Structural Star**	傷官 Hurting Officer
用神 **Useful God**	Ren 壬 Water
Conditions	The Earthly Branches forms a Water Structure. And Bing Fire happen to be missing from the chart. This person may suffer from poverty in life, no matter how learned or knowledgeable he or she may be.
Positive Circumstances	Bing Fire should, preferably, penetrate through the Heavenly Stems.
Negative Circumstances	Absence of Bing Fire.

* *Bing Fire and Ding Fire are the most-preferred Useful Gods.*

** *In a Zi (Rat) Month, Gui Water should be prevented from penetrating through the Heavenly Stems.*

十二月 Twelfth Month

Ox

| **Day Master** | Xin 辛 Metal | | **Month** | Chou 丑 (Ox) |

Summary

- Gui Water should be prevented from penetrating through the Heavenly Stems at all costs. This is because Gui Water in a Chou month appears as snow. And snow will also bury the Xin Metal.

- Where Ren Water is present but Bing Fire absent, this Xin Metal Day Master may suffer from loneliness, or even be inclined towards living a solitary, `hermit-like' life. Where Bing Fire is present in abundance but Ren Water is missing, this Xin Metal Day Master shall possess excellent business and financial acumen.

- Where Ren Water is absent and Bing Fire Present, there would be much joy and happiness in life. However, the success level of this person is mediocre at best. Much of his or her talents go unnoticed.

About Joey Yap

Joey Yap is the Founder and Master Trainer of the Mastery Academy of Chinese Metaphysics, a global organization devoted to the teaching of Feng Shui, BaZi, Mian Xiang and other Chinese Metaphysics subjects. He is also the Chief Consultant of Yap Global Consulting, an international consulting firm specialising in Feng Shui and Chinese Astrology services and audits.

He is the bestselling author of over 25 books, including *Stories and Lessons on Feng Shui, BaZi – The Destiny Code, Mian Xiang – Discover Face Reading, Feng Shui for Homebuyers Series*, and *Pure Feng Shui,* which was released by an international publisher.

He is also the producer of the first comprehensive reference source of Chinese Metaphysics, *The Chinese Metaphysics Compendium*, a compilation of all the essential formulas and applications known and practiced in Chinese Metaphysics today. He has since produced various other reference books and workbooks to aid students in their study and practice of Chinese Metaphysics subjects.

An avid proponent of technology being the way forward in disseminating knowledge of Chinese Metaphysics, Joey has developed, among others, the *BaZi Ming Pan 2.0 Software* and the *Xuan Kong Flying Stars Feng Shui Software*. This passion for fusing the best of modern technology with the best of classical studies lead him to create one of the pioneer online schools for Chinese Metaphysics education, the Mastery Academy E-Learning Centre (www.maelearning.com).

In addition to being a regular guest on various international radio and TV shows, Joey has also written columns for leading newspapers, as well as having contributed articles for various international magazines and publications. He has been featured in many popular publications and media including *Time International*, *Forbes International*, the *International Herald Tribune*, and Bloomberg TV, and was selected as one of Malaysia Tatler's 'Most Influential People in Malaysia' in 2008.

A naturally engaging speaker, Joey has presented to clients like Citibank, HSBC, IBM, Microsoft, Sime Darby, Bloomberg, HP, Samsung, Mah Sing, Nokia, Dijaya, and Standard Chartered.

Joey has also hosted his own TV series, *Discovering Feng Shui with Joey Yap*, and appeared on Malaysia's Astro TV network's *Walking the Dragons with Joey Yap*.

Joey's updates can be followed via Twitter at **www.twitter.com/joeyyap**. A full list of recent events and updates, and more information, can be found at **www.joeyyap.com** and **www.masteryacademy.com**

EDUCATION
The Mastery Academy of Chinese Metaphysics:
the first choice for practitioners and aspiring students of the art and science of Chinese Classical Feng Shui and Astrology.

For thousands of years, Eastern knowledge has been passed from one generation to another through the system of discipleship. A venerated master would accept suitable individuals at a young age as his disciples, and informally through the years, pass on his knowledge and skills to them. His disciples in turn, would take on their own disciples, as a means to perpetuate knowledge or skills.

This system served the purpose of restricting the transfer of knowledge to only worthy honourable individuals and ensuring that outsiders or Westerners would not have access to thousands of years of Eastern knowledge, learning and research.

However, the disciple system has also resulted in Chinese Metaphysics and Classical Studies lacking systematic teaching methods. Knowledge garnered over the years has not been accumulated in a concise, systematic manner, but scattered amongst practitioners, each practicing his/her knowledge, art and science, in isolation.

The disciple system, out of place in today's modern world, endangers the advancement of these classical fields that continue to have great relevance and application today.

At the Mastery Academy of Chinese Metaphysics, our Mission is to bring Eastern Classical knowledge in the fields of metaphysics, Feng Shui and Astrology sciences and the arts to the world. These Classical teachings and knowledge, previously shrouded in secrecy and passed on only through the discipleship system, are adapted into structured learning, which can easily be understood, learnt and mastered. Through modern learning methods, these renowned ancient arts, sciences and practices can be perpetuated while facilitating more extensive application and understanding of these classical subjects.

The Mastery Academy espouses an educational philosophy that draws from the best of the East and West. It is the world's premier educational institution for the study of Chinese Metaphysics Studies offering a wide range and variety of courses, ensuring that students have the opportunity to pursue their preferred field of study and enabling existing practitioners and professionals to gain cross-disciplinary knowledge that complements their current field of practice.

Courses at the Mastery Academy have been carefully designed to ensure a comprehensive yet compact syllabus. The modular nature of the courses enables students to immediately begin to put their knowledge into practice while pursuing continued study of their field and complementary fields. Students thus have the benefit of developing and gaining practical experience in tandem with the expansion and advancement of their theoretical knowledge.

Students can also choose from a variety of study options, from a distance learning program, the Homestudy Series, that enables study at one's own pace or intensive foundation courses and compact lecture-based courses, held in various cities around the world by Joey Yap or our licensed instructors. The Mastery Academy's faculty and make-up is international in nature, thus ensuring that prospective students can attend courses at destinations nearest to their country of origin or with a licensed Mastery Academy instructor in their home country.

The Mastery Academy provides 24x7 support to students through its Online Community, with a variety of tools, documents, forums and e-learning materials to help students stay at the forefront of research in their fields and gain invaluable assistance from peers and mentoring from their instructors.

TM

MASTERY ACADEMY
OF CHINESE METAPHYSICS

www.masteryacademy.com

MALAYSIA
19-3, The Boulevard
Mid Valley City
59200 Kuala Lumpur, Malaysia
Tel   : +603-2284 8080
Fax   : +603-2284 1218
Email : info@masteryacademy.com

SINGAPORE
14, Robinson Road # 13-00
Far East Finance Building
Singapore 048545
Tel   : +65-6494 9147
Email : singapore@masteryacademy.com

Australia, Austria, Canada, China, Croatia, Cyprus, Czech Republic, Denmark, France, Germany, Greece, Hungary, India, Italy, Kazakhstan, Malaysia, Netherlands (Holland), New Zealand, Philippines, Poland, Russian Federation, Singapore, Slovenia, South Africa, Switzerland, Turkey, U.S.A., Ukraine, United Kingdom

Introducing...
The Mastery Academy's E-Learning Center!

The Mastery Academy's goal has always been to share authentic knowledge of Chinese Metaphysics with the whole world.

Nevertheless, we do recognize that distance, time, and hotel and traveling costs – amongst many other factors – could actually hinder people from enrolling for a classroom-based course. But with the advent and amazing advance of IT today, NOT any more!

With this in mind, we have invested heavily in IT, to conceive what is probably the first and only E-Learning Center in the world today that offers a full range of studies in the field of Chinese Metaphysics.

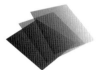

Convenient
Study from Your Own Home
Easy Enrollment

The Mastery Academy's E-Learning Center

Now, armed with your trusty computer or laptop, and Internet access, knowledge of classical Feng Shui, BaZi (Destiny Analysis) and Mian Xiang (Face Reading) are but a literal click away!

Study at your own pace, and interact with your Instructor and fellow students worldwide, from anywhere in the world. With our E-Learning Center, knowledge of Chinese Metaphysics is brought DIRECTLY to you in all its clarity – topic-by-topic, and lesson-by-lesson; with illustrated presentations and comprehensive notes expediting your learning curve!

Your education journey through our E-Learning Center may be done via any of the following approaches:

1. Online Courses

There are 3 Programs available: our Online Feng Shui Program, Online BaZi Program, and Online Mian Xiang Program. Each Program consists of several Levels, with each Level consisting of many Lessons in turn. Each Lesson contains a pre-recorded video session on the topic at hand, accompanied by presentation-slides and graphics as well as downloadable tutorial notes that you can print and file for future reference.

Video Lecture   Presentation   Downloadable
                          Slide   Notes

2. MA Live!

MA Live!, as its name implies, enables LIVE broadcasts of Joey Yap's courses and seminars – right to your computer screen. Students will not only get to see and hear Joey talk on real-time 'live', but also participate and more importantly, TALK to Joey via the MA Live! interface. All the benefits of a live class, minus the hassle of actually having to attend one!

How It Works

Our Live Classes   You at Home

3. Video-On-Demand (VOD)

Get immediate streaming-downloads of the Mastery Academy's wide range of educational DVDs, right on your computer screen. No more shipping costs and waiting time to be incurred!

**Instant VOD
Online**

Choose From Our list   Click "Play" on Your PC
of Available VODs!

Welcome to **www.maelearning.com**; the web portal of our E-Learning Center, and YOUR virtual gateway to Chinese Metaphysics!

Mastery Academy around the world

Canada

United States

Denmark

Czech Republic
Austria

United Kingdom

Switzerland

Poland

Netherlands
France
Italy
Cyprus

Germany
Solvenia
Hungary
Croatia
Greece

Russian
Federation

Ukraine

Turkey

Kazakhstan

India

China

South Africa

Philippines

Kuala Lumpur
Malaysia

Singapore

Australia

New Zealand

YAP GLOBAL CONSULTING

Joey Yap & Yap Global Consulting

Headed by Joey Yap, Yap Global Consulting (YGC) is a leading international consulting firm specializing in Feng Shui, Mian Xiang (Face Reading) and BaZi (Destiny Analysis) consulting services worldwide. Joey - an internationally renowned Master Trainer, Consultant, Speaker and best-selling Author - has dedicated his life to the art and science of Chinese Metaphysics.

YGC has its main offices in Kuala Lumpur and Australia, and draws upon its diverse reservoir of strength from a group of dedicated and experienced consultants based in more than 30 countries, worldwide.

As the pioneer in blending established, classical Chinese Metaphysics techniques with the latest approach in consultation practices, YGC has built its reputation on the principles of professionalism and only the highest standards of service. This allows us to retain the cutting edge in delivering Feng Shui and Destiny consultation services to both corporate and personal clients, in a simple and direct manner, without compromising on quality.

Across Industries: Our Portfolio of Clients

Our diverse portfolio of both corporate and individual clients from all around the world bears testimony to our experience and capabilities.

Virtually every industry imaginable has benefited from our services - ranging from academic and financial institutions, real-estate developers and multinational corporations, to those in the leisure and tourism industry. Our services are also engaged by professionals, prominent business personalities, celebrities, high-profile politicians and people from all walks of life.

YAP GLOBAL CONSULTING

Mr./Mrs./Ms.):

Details

_____ Fax: _____

ype of Consultation Are You Interested In?
☐ Shui ☐ BaZi ☐ Date Selection ☐ Yi Jing

ick if applicable:
e you a Property Developer looking to engage Yap Global nsulting?

e you a Property Investor looking for tailor-made packages uit your investment requirements?

Please attach your name card here.

Thank you for completing this form. Please fax it back to us at:

Singapore	Malaysia & the rest of the world
Tel : +65-6494 9147	Fax: +603-2284 2213 Tel : +603-2284 1213

Feng Shui Consultations

For Residential Properties
- Initial Land/Property Assessment
- Residential Feng Shui Consultations
- Residential Land Selection
- End-to-End Residential Consultation

For Commercial Properties
- Initial Land/Property Assessment
- Commercial Feng Shui Consultations
- Commercial Land Selection
- End-to-End Commercial Consultation

For Property Developers
- End-to-End Consultation
- Post-Consultation Advisory Services
- Panel Feng Shui Consultant

For Property Investors
- Your Personal Feng Shui Consultant
- Tailor-Made Packages

For Memorial Parks & Burial Sites
- Yin House Feng Shui

BaZi Consultations

Personal Destiny Analysis
- Personal Destiny Analysis for Individuals
- Children's BaZi Analysis
- Family BaZi Analysis

Strategic Analysis for Corporate Organizations
- Corporate BaZi Consultations
- BaZi Analysis for Human Resource Management

Entrepreneurs & Business Owners
- BaZi Analysis for Entrepreneurs

Career Pursuits
- BaZi Career Analysis

Relationships
- Marriage and Compatibility Analysis
- Partnership Analysis

For Everyone
- Annual BaZi Forecast
- Your Personal BaZi Coach**Personal Destiny Analysis**
- Personal Destiny Analysis for Individuals

Date Selection Consultations

- **Marriage Date Selection**
- **Caesarean Birth Date Selection**
- **House-Moving Date Selection**
- **Renovation & Groundbreaking Dates**

- **Signing of Contracts**
- **Official Openings**
- **Product Launches**

Yi Jing Assessment

A Time-Tested, Accurate Science

- With a history predating 4 millennia, the Yi Jing - or Classic of Change - is one of the oldest Chinese texts surviving today. Its purpose as an oracle, in predicting the outcome of things, is based on the variables of Time, Space and Specific Events.

- A Yi Jing Assessment provides specific answers to any specific questions you may have about a specific event or endeavor. This is something that a Destiny Analysis would not be able to give you.

Basically, what a Yi Jing Assessment does is focus on only ONE aspect or item at a particular point in your life, and give you a calculated prediction of the details that will follow suit, if you undertake a particular action. It gives you an insight into a situation, and what course of action to take in order to arrive at a satisfactory outcome at the end of the day.

Please Contact YGC for a personalized Yi Jing Assessment!

INVITING US TO YOUR CORPORATE EVENTS

Many reputable organizations and institutions have worked closely with YGC to build a synergistic business relationship by engaging our team of consultants, led by Joey Yap, as speakers at their corporate events. Our seminars and short talks are always packed with audiences consisting of clients and associates of multinational and public-listed companies as well as key stakeholders of financial institutions.

We tailor our seminars and talks to suit the anticipated or pertinent group of audience. Be it a department, subsidiary, your clients or even the entire corporation, we aim to fit your requirements in delivering the intended message(s).

CHINESE METAPHYSICS REFERENCE SERIES

The Chinese Metaphysics Reference Series is a collection of reference texts, source material, and educational textbooks to be used as supplementary guides by scholars, students, researchers, teachers and practitioners of Chinese Metaphysics.

These comprehensive and structured books provide fast, easy reference to aid in the study and practice of various Chinese Metaphysics subjects including Feng Shui, BaZi, Yi Jing, Zi Wei, Liu Ren, Ze Ri, Ta Yi, Qi Men and Mian Xiang.

The Chinese Metaphysics Compendium

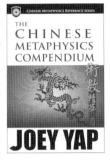

At over 1,000 pages, the *Chinese Metaphysics Compendium* is a unique one-volume reference book that compiles all the formulas relating to Feng Shui, BaZi (Four Pillars of Destiny), Zi Wei (Purple Star Astrology), Yi Jing (I-Ching), Qi Men (Mystical Doorways), Ze Ri (Date Selection), Mian Xiang (Face Reading) and other sources of Chinese Metaphysics.

It is presented in the form of easy-to-read tables, diagrams and reference charts, all of which are compiled into one handy book. This first-of-its-kind compendium is presented in both English and the original Chinese, so that none of the meanings and contexts of the technical terminologies are lost.

The only essential and comprehensive reference on Chinese Metaphysics, and an absolute must-have for all students, scholars, and practitioners of Chinese Metaphysics.

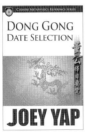

Dong Gong Date
Selection

Xuan Kong Da Gua Ten
Thousand Year Calendar

Xuan Kong Da Gua
Reference Book

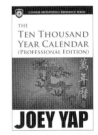

The Ten Thousand Year
Calendar *(Professional
Edition)*

San Yuan Dragon Gate
Eight Formations Water
Method

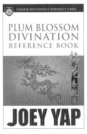

Plum Blossoms
Divination Reference
Book

Qi Men Dun Jia
1080 Charts

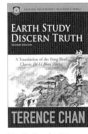

Earth Study Discern
Truth Volume Two

Educational Tools & Software

Xuan Kong Flying Stars Feng Shui Software
The Essential Application for Enthusiasts and Professionals

The Xuan Kong Flying Stars Feng Shui Software is a brand-new application by Joey Yap that will assist you in the practice of Xuan Kong Feng Shui with minimum fuss and maximum effectiveness. Superimpose the Flying Stars charts over your house plans (or those of your clients) to clearly demarcate the 9 Palaces. Use it to help you create fast and sophisticated chart drawings and presentations, as well as to assist professional practitioners in the report-writing process before presenting the final reports for your clients. Students can use it to practice their Xuan Kong Feng Shui skills and knowledge, and it can even be used by designers and architects!

Some of the highlights of the software include:
- Natal Flying Stars
- Monthly Flying Stars
- 81 Flying Stars Combinations
- Dual-View Format
- Annual Flying Stars
- Flying Stars Integration
- 24 Mountains

All charts will be are printable and configurable, and can be saved for future editing. Also, you'll be able to export your charts into most image file formats like jpeg, bmp, and gif.

The Xuan Kong Flying Stars Feng Shui Software can make your Feng Shui practice simpler and more effective, garnering you amazing results with less effort!

Mini Feng Shui Compass

This Mini Feng Shui Compass with the accompanying Companion Booklet written by leading Feng Shui and Chinese Astrology Master Trainer Joey Yap is a must-have for any Feng Shui enthusiast.

The Mini Feng Shui Compass is a self-aligning compass that is not only light at 100gms but also built sturdily to ensure it will be convenient to use anywhere. The rings on the Mini Feng Shui Compass are bi-lingual and incorporate the 24 Mountain Rings that is used in your traditional Luo Pan.

The comprehensive booklet included will guide you in applying the 24 Mountain Directions on your Mini Feng Shui Compass effectively and the 8 Mansions Feng Shui to locate the most auspicious locations within your home, office and surroundings. You can also use the Mini Feng Shui Compass when measuring the direction of your property for the purpose of applying Flying Stars Feng Shui.

Educational Tools & Software

BaZi Ming Pan Software Version 2.0
Professional Four Pillars Calculator for Destiny Analysis

The BaZi Ming Pan Version 2.0 Professional Four Pillars Calculator for Destiny Analysis is the most technically advanced software of its kind in the world today. It allows even those without any knowledge of BaZi to generate their own BaZi Charts, and provides virtually every detail required to undertake a comprehensive Destiny Analysis.

This Professional Four Pillars Calculator allows you to even undertake a day-to-day analysis of your Destiny. What's more, all BaZi Charts generated by this software are fully printable and configurable! Designed for both enthusiasts and professional practitioners, this state-of-the-art software blends details with simplicity, and is capable of generating 4 different types of BaZi charts: **BaZi Professional Charts, BaZi Annual Analysis Charts, BaZi Pillar Analysis Charts and BaZi Family Relationship Charts.**

Additional references, configurable to cater to all levels of BaZi knowledge and usage, include:
• Dual Age & Bilingual Option (Western & Chinese) • Na Yin narrations • 12 Life Stages evaluation • Death & Emptiness • Gods & Killings • Special Days • Heavenly Virtue Nobles

This software also comes with a Client Management feature that allows you to save and trace clients' records instantly, navigate effortlessly between BaZi charts, and file your clients' information in an organized manner.

The BaZi Ming Pan Version 2.0 Calculator sets a new standard by combining the best of BaZi and technology.

Joey Yap Feng Shui Template Set

Directions are the cornerstone of any successful Feng Shui audit or application. The **Joey Yap Feng Shui Template Set** is a set of three templates to simplify the process of taking directions and determining locations and positions, whether it's for a building, a house, or an open area such as a plot of land, all with just a floor plan or area map.

The Set comprises 3 basic templates: The Basic Feng Shui Template, 8 Mansions Feng Shui Template, and the Flying Stars Feng Shui Template.

With bi-lingual notations for these directions; both in English and the original Chinese, the **Joey Yap Feng Shui Template Set** comes with its own Booklet that gives simple yet detailed instructions on how to make use of the 3 templates within.

• Easy-to-use, simple, and straightforward
• Small and portable; each template measuring only 5" x 5"
• Additional 8 Mansions and Flying Stars Reference Rings
• Handy companion booklet with usage tips and examples

Accelerate Your Face Reading Skills With Joey Yap's Face Reading Revealed DVD Series

Mian Xiang, the Chinese art of Face Reading, is an ancient form of physiognomy and entails the use of the face and facial characteristics to evaluate key aspects of a person's life, luck and destiny. In his Face Reading DVDs series, Joey Yap shows you how the facial features reveal a wealth of information about a person's luck, destiny and personality.

Mian Xiang also tell us the talents, quirks and personality of an individual. Do you know that just by looking at a person's face, you can ascertain his or her health, wealth, relationships and career? Let Joey Yap show you how the 12 Palaces can be utilised to reveal a person's inner talents, characteristics and much more.

Each facial feature on the face represents one year in a person's life. Your face is a 100-year map of your life and each position reveals your fortune and destiny at a particular age as well as insights and information about your personality, skills, abilities and destiny.

Using Mian Xiang, you will also be able to plan your life ahead by identifying, for example, the right business partner and knowing the sort of person that you need to avoid. By knowing their characteristics through the facial features, you will be able to gauge their intentions and gain an upper hand in negotiations.

Do you know what moles signify? Do they bring good or bad luck? Do you want to build better relationships with your partner or family members or have your ever wondered why you seem to be always bogged down by trivial problems in your life?

In these highly entertaining DVDs, Joey will help you answer all these questions and more. You will be able to ascertain the underlying meaning of moles, birthmarks or even the type of your hair in Face Reading. Joey will also reveal the guidelines to help you foster better and stronger relationships with your loved ones through Mian Xiang.

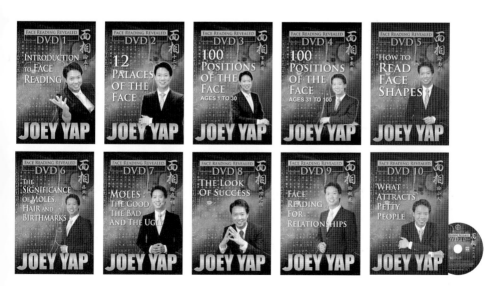

Feng Shui for Homebuyers DVD Series

Best-selling Author, and international Master Trainer and Consultant Joey Yap reveals in these DVDs the significant Feng Shui features that every homebuyer should know when evaluating a property.

Joey will guide you on how to customise your home to maximise the Feng Shui potential of your property and gain the full benefit of improving your health, wealth and love life using the 9 Palace Grid. He will show you how to go about applying the classical applications of the Life Gua and House Gua techniques to get attuned to your Sheng Qi (positive energies).

In these DVDs, you will also learn how to identify properties with good Feng Shui features that will help you promote a fulfilling life and achieve your full potential. Discover how to avoid properties with negative Feng Shui that can bring about detrimental effects to your health, wealth and relationships.

Joey will also elaborate on how to fix the various aspects of your home that may have an impact on the Feng Shui of your property and give pointers on how to tap into the positive energies to support your goals.

Discover Feng Shui with Joey Yap (TV Series)

Discover Feng Shui with Joey Yap: Set of 4 DVDs

Informative and entertaining, classical Feng Shui comes alive in *Discover Feng Shui with Joey Yap!*

Dying to know how you can use Feng Shui to improve your house or office, but simply too busy attend for formal classes?

You have the questions. Now let Joey personally answer them in this 4-set DVD compilation! Learn how to ensure the viability of your residence or workplace, Feng Shui-wise, without having to convert it into a Chinese antiques' shop. Classical Feng Shui is about harnessing the natural power of your environment to improve quality of life. It's a systematic and subtle metaphysical science.

And that's not all. Joey also debunks many a myth about classical Feng Shui, and shares with viewers Face Reading tips as well!

Own the series that national channel 8TV did a re-run of in 2005, today!

Annual Releases

Chinese Astrology for 2009

This information-packed annual guide to the Chinese Astrology for 2009 goes way beyond the conventional 'animal horoscope' book. To begin with, author Joey Yap includes a personalized outlook for 2009 based on the individual's BaZi Day Pillar (Jia Zi) and a 12-month micro-analysis for each of the 60 Day Pillars – in addition to the annual outlook for all 12 animal signs and the 12-month outlook for each animal sign in 2009. Find out what awaits you in 2009 from the four key aspects of Health, Wealth, Career and Relationships...with Joey Yap's **Chinese Astrology for 2009**!

Feng Shui for 2009

Maximize the Qi of the Year of the Earth Rat for your home and office, with Joey Yap's **Feng Shui for 2009** book. Learn how to tap into the positive sectors of the year, and avoid the negative ones and those with the Annual Afflictions, as well as ascertain how the annual Flying Stars affect your property by comparing them against the Eight Mansions (Ba Zhai) for 2009. Flying Stars enthusiasts will also find this book handy, as it includes the monthly Flying Stars charts for the year, accompanied by detailed commentaries on what sectors to use and avoid – to enable you to optimize your Academic, Relationships and Wealth Luck in 2009.

Tong Shu Diary 2009

Organize your professional and personal lives with the **Tong Shu Diary 2009**, with a twist... it also allows you to determine the most suitable dates on which you can undertake important activities and endeavors throughout the year! This compact Diary integrates the Chinese Solar and Lunar Calendars with the universal lingua franca of the Gregorian Calendar.

Tong Shu Monthly Planner 2009

Tailor-made for the Feng Shui or BaZi enthusiast in you, or even professional Chinese Metaphysics consultants who want a compact planner with useful information incorporated into it. In the **Tong Shu Monthly Planner 2009**, you will find the auspicious and inauspicious dates for the year marked out for you, alongside the most suitable activities to be undertaken on each day. As a bonus, there is also a reference section containing all the monthly Flying Stars charts and Annual Afflictions for 2009.

Tong Shu Desktop Calendar 2009

Get an instant snapshot of the suitable and unsuitable activities for each day of the Year of the Earth Rat, with the icons displayed on this lightweight Desktop Calendar. Elegantly presenting the details of the Chinese Solar Calendar in the form of the standard Gregorian one, the **Tong Shu Desktop Calendar 2009** is perfect for Chinese Metaphysics enthusiasts and practitioners alike. Whether it a business launching or meeting, ground breaking ceremony, travel or house-moving that you have in mind, this Calendar is designed to fulfill your information needs.

Tong Shu Year Planner 2009

This one-piece Planner presents you all the essential information you need for significant activities or endeavors...with just a quick glance! In a nutshell, it allows you to identify the favorable and unfavorable days, which will in turn enable you to schedule your year's activities so as to make the most of good days, and avoid the ill-effects brought about by inauspicious ones.

Continue Your Journey with Joey Yap's Books

Walking the Dragons

Walking the Dragons is a guided tour through the classical landform Feng Shui of ancient China, an enchanting collection of deeply-researched yet entertaining essays rich in historical detail.

Compiled in one book for the first time from Joey Yap's Feng Shui Mastery Excursion Series, the book highlights China's extensive, vibrant history with astute observations on the Feng Shui of important sites and places. Learn the landform formations of Yin Houses (tombs and burial places), as well as mountains, temples, castles, and villages.

It demonstrates complex Feng Shui theories and principles in easy-to-understand, entertaining language and is the perfect addition to the bookshelf of a Feng Shui or history lover. Anyone, whether experienced in Feng Shui or new to the practice, will be able to enjoy the insights shared in this book. Complete with gorgeous full-colour pictures of all the amazing sights and scenery, it's the next best thing to having been there yourself!

Your Aquarium Here

Your Aquarium Here is a simple, practical, hands-on Feng Shui book that teaches you how to incorporate a Water feature – an aquarium – for optimal Feng Shui benefit, whether for personal relationships, wealth, or career. Designed to be comprehensive yet simple enough for a novice or beginner, *Your Aquarium Here* provides historical and factual information about the role of Water in Feng Shui, and provides a step-by-step guide to installing and using an aquarium.

The book is the first in the **Fengshuilogy Series**, a series of matter-of-fact and useful Feng Shui books designed for the person who wants to do fuss-free Feng Shui. Not everyone who wants to use Feng Shui is an expert or a scholar! This series of books are just the kind you'd want on your bookshelf to gain basic, practical knowledge of the subject. Go ahead and Feng Shui-It-Yourself – *Your Aquarium Here* eliminates all the fuss and bother, but maintains all the fun and excitement, of authentic Feng Shui application!

The Art of Date Selection: Personal Date Selection

In today's modern world, it is not good enough to just do things effectively – we need to do them efficiently, as well. From the signing of business contracts and moving into a new home, to launching a product or even tying the knot; everything has to move, and move very quickly too. There is a premium on Time, where mistakes can indeed be costly.

The notion of doing the Right Thing, at the Right Time and in the Right Place is the very backbone of Date Selection. Because by selecting a suitable date specially tailored to a specific activity or endeavor, we infuse it with the most positive energies prevalent in our environment during that particular point in time; and that could well make the difference between 'make-and-break'! With the *Art of Date Selection: Personal Date Selection*, learn simple, practical methods you can employ to select not just good dates, but personalized good dates. Whether it's a personal activity such as a marriage or professional endeavor such as launching a business, signing a contract or even acquiring assets, this book will show you how to pick the good dates and tailor them to suit the activity in question, as well as avoid the negative ones too!

The Art of Date Selection: Feng Shui Date Selection

Date Selection is the Art of selecting the most suitable date, where the energies present on the day support the specific activities or endeavors we choose to undertake on that day. Feng Shui is the Chinese Metaphysical study of the Physiognomy of the Land – landforms and the Qi they produce, circulate and conduct. Hence, anything that exists on this Earth is invariably subject to the laws of Feng Shui. So what do we get when Date Selection and Feng Shui converge?

Feng Shui Date Selection, of course! Say you wish to renovate your home, or maybe buy or rent one. Or perhaps, you're a developer, and wish to know WHEN is the best date possible to commence construction works on your project. In any case – and all cases – you certainly wish to ensure that your endeavors are well supported by the positive energies present on a good day, won't you? And this is where Date Selection supplements the practice of Feng Shui. At the end of the day, it's all about making the most of what's good, and minimizing what's bad.

(Available Soon)

Continue Your Journey with Joey Yap's Books

Feng Shui For Homebuyers - Exterior

Best selling Author and international Feng Shui Consultant, Joey Yap, will guide you on the various important features in your external environment that have a bearing on the Feng Shui of your home. For homeowners, those looking to build their own home or even investors who are looking to apply Feng Shui to their homes, this book provides valuable information from the classical Feng Shui theories and applications.

This book will assist you in screening and eliminating unsuitable options with negative FSQ (Feng Shui Quotient) should you acquire your own land or if you are purchasing a newly built home. It will also help you in determining which plot of land to select and which to avoid when purchasing an empty parcel of land.

Feng Shui for Homebuyers - Interior

A book every homeowner or potential house buyer should have. The Feng Shui for Homebuyers (Interior) is an informative reference book and invaluable guide written by best selling Author and international Feng Shui Consultant, Joey Yap.

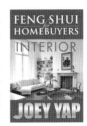

This book provides answers to the important questions of what really does matter when looking at the internal Feng Shui of a home or office. It teaches you how to analyze your home or office floor plans and how to improve their Feng Shui. It will answer all your questions about the positive and negative flow of Qi within your home and ways to utilize them to your maximum benefit.

Providing you with a guide to calculating your Life Gua and House Gua to fine-tune your Feng Shui within your property, Joey Yap focuses on practical, easily applicable ideas on what you can implement internally in a property.

Feng Shui for Apartment Buyers - Home Owners

Finding a good apartment or condominium is never an easy task but who do you ensure that is also has good Feng Shui? And how exactly do you apply Feng Shui to an apartment or condominium or high-rise residence?

These questions and more are answered by renowned Feng Shui Consultant and Master Trainer Joey Yap in **Feng Shui for Apartment Buyers - Home Owners**. Joey answers the key questions about Feng Shui and apartments, then guides you through the bare basics like taking a direction and super-imposing a Flying Stars chart onto a floor plan. Joey also walks you through the process of finding an apartment with favorable Feng Shui, sharing with you some of the key methods and techniques that are employed by professional Feng Shui consultants in assesing apartment Feng Shui.

In his trademark straight-to-the-point manner, Joey shares with you the Feng Shui do's and dont's when it comes to finding an apartment with favorable Feng Shui and which is conducive for home living.

The Ten Thousand Year Calendar

The Ten Thousand Year Calendar or 萬年曆 Wan Nian Li is a regular reference book and an invaluable tool used by masters, practitioners and students of Feng Shui, BaZi (Four Pillars of Destiny), Chinese Zi Wei Dou Shu Astrology (Purple Star), Yi Jing (I-Ching) and Date Selection specialists.

JOEY YAP's Ten Thousand Year Calendar provides the Gregorian (Western) dates converted into both the Chinese Solar and Lunar calendar in both the English and Chinese language.

It also includes a comprehensive set of key Feng Shui and Chinese Astrology charts and references, including Xuan Kong Nine Palace Flying Star Charts, Monthly and Daily Flying Stars, Water Dragon Formulas Reference Charts, Zi Wei Dou Shu (Purple Star) Astrology Reference Charts, BaZi (Four Pillars of Destiny) Heavenly Stems, Earthly Branches and all other related reference tables for Chinese Metaphysical Studies.

Continue Your Journey with Joey Yap's Books

Stories and Lessons on Feng Shui (English & Chinese versions)

Stories and Lessons on Feng Shui is a compilation of essays and stories written by leading Feng Shui and Chinese Astrology trainer and consultant Joey Yap about Feng Shui and Chinese Astrology.

In this heart-warming collection of easy to read stories, find out why it's a myth that you should never have Water on the right hand side of your house, the truth behind the infamous 'love' and 'wealth' corners and that the sudden death of a pet fish is really NOT due to bad luck!

More Stories and Lessons on Feng Shui

Finally, the long-awaited sequel to *Stories & Lessons on Feng Shui*!

If you've read the best-selling Stories & Lessons on Feng Shui, you won't want to miss this book. And even if you haven't read *Stories & Lessons on Feng Shui*, there's always a time to rev your Feng Shui engine up.

The time is NOW.

And the book? *More Stories & Lessons on Feng Shui* – the 2nd compilation of the most popular articles and columns penned by Joey Yap; **specially featured in national and international publications, magazines and newspapers.**

All in all, *More Stories & Lessons on Feng Shui* is a delightful chronicle of Joey's articles, thoughts and vast experience - as a professional Feng Shui consultant and instructor - that have been purposely refined, edited and expanded upon to make for a light-hearted, interesting yet educational read. And with Feng Shui, BaZi, Mian Xiang and Yi Jing all thrown into this one dish, there's something for everyone…so all you need to serve or accompany *More Stories & Lessons on Feng Shui* with is your favorite cup of tea or coffee!

Even More Stories and Lessons on Feng Shui

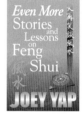

In this third release in the Stories and Lessons series, Joey Yap continues his exploration on the study and practice of Feng Shui in the modern age through a series of essays and personal anecdotes. Debunking superstition, offering simple and understandable "Feng Shui-It-Yourself" tips, and expounding on the history and origins of classical Feng Shui, Joey takes readers on a journey that is always refreshing and exciting.

Besides 'behind-the-scenes' revelations of actual Feng Shui audits, there are also chapters on how beginners can easily and accurately incorporate Feng Shui practice into their lives, as well as travel articles that offer proof that when it comes to Feng Shui, the Qi literally knows no boundaries.

In his trademark lucid and forthright style, Joey covers themes and topics that will strike a chord with all readers who have an interest in Feng Shui.

Mian Xiang - Discover Face Reading

Need to identify a suitable business partner? How about understanding your staff or superiors better? Or even choosing a suitable spouse? These mind boggling questions can be answered in Joey Yap's introductory book to Face Reading titled *Mian Xiang – Discover Face Reading*. This book will help you discover the hidden secrets in a person's face.

Mian Xiang – Discover Face Reading is comprehensive book on all areas of Face Reading, covering some of the most important facial features, including the forehead, mouth, ears and even the philtrum above your lips. This book will help you analyse not just your Destiny but help you achieve your full potential and achieve life fulfillment.

Continue Your Journey with Joey Yap's Books

BaZi - The Destiny Code (English & Chinese versions)

Leading Chinese Astrology Master Trainer Joey Yap makes it easy to learn how to unlock your Destiny through your BaZi with this book. BaZi or Four Pillars of Destiny is an ancient Chinese science which enables individuals to understand their personality, hidden talents and abilities as well as their luck cycle, simply by examining the information contained within their birth data. *The Destiny Code* is the first book that shows readers how to plot and interpret their own Destiny charts and lays the foundation for more in-depth BaZi studies. Written in a lively entertaining style, the Destiny Code makes BaZi accessible to the layperson. Within 10 chapters, understand and appreciate more about this astoundingly accurate ancient Chinese Metaphysical science.

BaZi - The Destiny Code Revealed

In this follow up to Joey Yap's best-selling *The Destiny Code*, delve deeper into your own Destiny chart through an understanding of the key elemental relationships that affect the Heavenly Stems and Earthly Branches. Find out how Combinations, Clash, Harm, Destructions and Punishments bring new dimension to a BaZi chart. Complemented by extensive real-life examples, *The Destiny Code Revealed* takes you to the next level of BaZi, showing you how to unlock the Codes of Destiny and to take decisive action at the right time, and capitalise on the opportunities in life.

Xuan Kong: Flying Stars Feng Shui

Xuan Kong Flying Stars Feng Shui is an essential introductory book to the subject of Xuan Kong Fei Xing, a well-known and popular system of Feng Shui, written by International Feng Shui Master Trainer Joey Yap.

In his down-to-earth, entertaining and easy to read style, Joey Yap takes you through the essential basics of Classical Feng Shui, and the key concepts of Xuan Kong Fei Xing (Flying Stars). Learn how to fly the stars, plot a Flying Star chart for your home or office and interpret the stars and star combinations. Find out how to utilise the favourable areas of your home or office for maximum benefit and learn 'tricks of the trade' and 'trade secrets' used by Feng Shui practitioners to enhance and maximise Qi in your home or office.

An essential integral introduction to the subject of Classical Feng Shui and the Flying Stars System of Feng Shui!

Xuan Kong Flying Stars: Structures and Combinations

Delve deeper into Flying Stars through a greater understanding of the 81 Combinations and the influence of the Annual and Monthly Stars on the Base, Sitting and Facing Stars in this 2nd book of the Xuan Kong Feng Shui series. Learn how Structures like the Combination of 10, Up the Mountain and Down the River, Pearl and Parent String Structures are used to interpret a Flying Star chart.

(Available Soon)

Xuan Kong Flying Stars: Advanced Techniques

Take your knowledge of Xuan Kong Flying Stars to a higher level and learn how to apply complex techniques and advanced formulas such as Castle Gate Technique, Seven Star Robbery Formation, Advancing the Dragon Formation and Replacement Star technique amongst others. Joey Yap shows you how to use the Life Palace technique to combine Gua Numbers with Flying Star numbers and utilise the predictive facets of Flying Stars Feng Shui.

(Available Soon)

Elevate Your Feng Shui Skills With Joey Yap's Home Study Course And Educational DVDs

Xuan Kong Vol.1
An Advanced Feng Shui Home Study Course

Learn the Xuan Kong Flying Star Feng Shui system in just 20 lessons! Joey Yap's specialised notes and course work have been written to enable distance learning without compromising on the breadth or quality of the syllabus. Learn at your own pace with the same material students in a live class would use. The most comprehensive distance learning course on Xuan Kong Flying Star Feng Shui in the market. Xuan Kong Flying Star Vol.1 comes complete with a special binder for all your course notes.

Feng Shui for Period 8 - (DVD)

Don't miss the Feng Shui Event of the next 20 years! Catch Joey Yap LIVE and find out just what Period 8 is all about. This DVD boxed set zips you through the fundamentals of Feng Shui and the impact of this important change in the Feng Shui calendar. Joey's entertaining, conversational style walks you through the key changes that Period 8 will bring and how to tap into Wealth Qi and Good Feng Shui for the next 20 years.

Xuan Kong Flying Stars Beginners Workshop - (DVD)

Take a front row seat in Joey Yap's Xuan Kong Flying Stars workshop with this unique LIVE RECORDING of Joey Yap's Xuan Kong Flying Stars Feng Shui workshop, attended by over 500 people. This DVD program provides an effective and quick introduction of Xuan Kong Feng Shui essentials for those who are just starting out in their study of classical Feng Shui. Learn to plot your own Flying Star chart in just 3 hours. Learn 'trade secret' methods, remedies and cures for Flying Stars Feng Shui. This boxed set contains 3 DVDs and 1 workbook with notes and charts for reference.

BaZi Four Pillars of Destiny Beginners Workshop - (DVD)

Ever wondered what Destiny has in store for you? Or curious to know how you can learn more about your personality and inner talents? BaZi or Four Pillars of Destiny is an ancient Chinese science that enables us to understand a person's hidden talent, inner potential, personality, health and wealth luck from just their birth data. This specially compiled DVD set of Joey Yap's BaZi Beginners Workshop provides a thorough and comprehensive introduction to BaZi. Learn how to read your own chart and understand your own luck cycle. This boxed set contains 3 DVDs and 1 workbook with notes and reference charts.

Interested in learning MORE about Feng Shui? Advance Your Feng Shui Knowledge with the Mastery Academy Courses.

Feng Shui Mastery Series™
LIVE COURSES (MODULES ONE TO FOUR)

Feng Shui Mastery – Module One
Beginners Course

Designed for students seeking an entry-level intensive program into the study of Feng Shui , Module One is an intensive foundation course that aims not only to provide you with an introduction to Feng Shui theories and formulas and equip you with the skills and judgments to begin practicing and conduct simple Feng Shui audits upon successful completion of the course. Learn all about Forms, Eight Mansions Feng Shui and Flying Star Feng Shui in just one day with a unique, structured learning program that makes learning Feng Shui quick and easy!

Feng Shui Mastery – Module Two
Practitioners Course

Building on the knowledge and foundation in classical Feng Shui theory garnered in M1, M2 provides a more advanced and in-depth understanding of Eight Mansions, Xuan Kong Flying Star and San He and introduces students to theories that are found only in the classical Chinese Feng Shui texts. This 3-Day Intensive course hones analytical and judgment skills, refines Luo Pan (Chinese Feng Shui compass) skills and reveals 'trade secret' remedies. Module Two covers advanced Forms Analysis, San He's Five Ghost Carry Treasure formula, Advanced Eight Mansions and Xuan Kong Flying Stars and equips you with the skills needed to undertake audits and consultations for residences and offices.

Feng Shui Mastery – Module Three
Advanced Practitioners Course

Module Three is designed for Professional Feng Shui Practitioners. Learn advanced topics in Feng Shui and take your skills to a cutting edge level. Be equipped with the knowledge, techniques and confidence to conduct large scale audits (like estate and resort planning). Learn how to apply different systems appropriately to remedy situations or cases deemed inauspicious by one system and reconcile conflicts in different systems of Feng Shui. Gain advanced knowledge of San He (Three Harmony) systems and San Yuan (Three Cycles) systems, advanced Luan Tou (Forms Feng Shui) and specialist Water Formulas.

Feng Shui Mastery – Module Four
Master Course

The graduating course of the Feng Shui Mastery (FSM) Series, this course takes the advanced practitioner to the Master level. Power packed M4 trains students to 'walk the mountains' and identify superior landform, superior grade structures and make qualitative evaluations of landform, structures, Water and Qi and covers advanced and exclusive topics of San He, San Yuan, Xuan Kong, Ba Zhai, Luan Tou (Advanced Forms and Water Formula) Feng Shui. Master Internal, External and Luan Tou (Landform) Feng Shui methodologies to apply Feng Shui at every level and undertake consultations of every scale and magnitude, from houses and apartments to housing estates, townships, shopping malls and commercial districts.

BaZi Mastery – Module One
Intensive Foundation Course

This Intensive One Day Foundation Course provides an introduction to the principles and fundamentals of BaZi (Four Pillars of Destiny) and Destiny Analysis methods such as Ten Gods, Useful God and Strength of Qi. Learn how to plot a BaZi chart and interpret your Destiny and your potential. Master BaZi and learn to capitalize on your strengths, minimize risks and downturns and take charge of your Destiny.

BaZi Mastery – Module Two
Practical BaZi Applications

BaZi Module Two teaches students advanced BaZi analysis techniques and specific analysis methods for relationship luck, health evaluation, wealth potential and career potential. Students will learn to identify BaZi chart structures, sophisticated methods for applying the Ten Gods, and how to read Auxiliary Stars. Students who have completed Module Two will be able to conduct professional BaZi readings.

BaZi Mastery – Module Three
Advanced Practitioners Program

Designed for the BaZi practitioner, learn how to read complex cases and unique events in BaZi charts and perform Big and Small assessments. Discover how to analyze personalities and evaluate talents precisely, as well as special formulas and classical methodologies for BaZi from classics such as Di Tian Sui and Qiong Tong Bao Jian.

BaZi Mastery – Module Four
Master Course in BaZi

The graduating course of the BaZi Mastery Series, this course takes the advanced practitioner to the Masters' level. BaZi M4 focuses on specialized techniques of BaZi reading, unique special structures and advance methods from ancient classical texts. This program includes techniques on date selection and ancient methodologies from the Qiong Tong Bao Jian and Yuan Hai Zi Ping classics.

Xuan Kong Mastery – Module One
Advanced Foundation Program

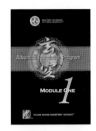

This course is for the experienced Feng Shui professionals who wish to expand their knowledge and skills in the Xuan Kong system of Feng Shui, covering important foundation methods and techniques from the Wu Chang and Guang Dong lineages of Xuan Kong Feng Shui.

Xuan Kong Mastery – Module Two A
Advanced Xuan Kong Methodologies

Designed for Feng Shui practitioners seeking to specialise in the Xuan Kong system, this program focuses on methods of application and Joey Yap's unique Life Palace and Shifting Palace Methods, as well as methods and techniques from the Wu Chang lineage.

Xuan Kong Mastery – Module Two B
Purple White

Explore in detail and in great depth the star combinations in Xuan Kong. Learn how each different combination reacts or responds in different palaces, under different environmental circumstances and to whom in the property. Learn methods, theories and techniques extracted from ancient classics such as Xuan Kong Mi Zhi, Xuan Kong Fu, Fei Xing Fu and Zi Bai Jue.

Xuan Kong Mastery – Module Three
Advanced Xuan Kong Da Gua

This intensive course focuses solely on the Xuan Kong Da Gua system covering the theories, techniques and methods of application of this unique 64-Hexagram based system of Xuan Kong including Xuan Kong Da Gua for landform analysis.

Walk the Mountains! Learn Feng Shui in a Practical and Hands-on Program

---

Feng Shui Mastery Excursion Series™ : CHINA

Learn landform (Luan Tou) Feng Shui by walking the mountains and chasing the Dragon's vein in China. This Program takes the students in a study tour to examine notable Feng Shui landmarks, mountains, hills, valleys, ancient palaces, famous mansions, houses and tombs in China. The Excursion is a 'practical' hands-on course where students are shown to perform readings using the formulas they've learnt and to recognize and read Feng Shui Landform (Luan Tou) formations.

Read about China Excursion here:
http://www.masteryacademy.com/Education/schoolfengshui/fengshuimasteryexcursion.asp

Mian Xiang Mastery Series™
LIVE COURSES (MODULES ONE AND TWO)

Mian Xiang Mastery – Module One
Basic Face Reading

A person's face is their fortune – learn more about the ancient Chinese art of Face Reading. In just one day, be equipped with techniques and skills to read a person's face and ascertain their character, luck, wealth and relationship luck.

Mian Xiang Mastery – Module Two
Practical Face Reading

Mian Xiang Module Two covers face reading techniques extracted from the ancient classics Shen Xiang Quan Pian and Shen Xiang Tie Guan Dau. Gain a greater depth and understanding of Mian Xiang and learn to recognize key structures and characteristics in a person's face.

Yi Jing Mastery Series™
LIVE COURSES (MODULES ONE AND TWO)

Yi Jing Mastery – Module One
Traditional Yi Jing

'Yi', relates to change. Change is the only constant in life and the universe, without exception to this rule. The Yi Jing is hence popularly referred to as the Book or Classic of Change. Discoursed in the language of Yin and Yang, the Yi Jing is one of the oldest Chinese classical texts surviving today. With Traditional Yi Jing, learnn how this Classic is used to divine the outcomes of virtually every facet of life; from your relationships to seeking an answer to the issues you may face in your daily life.

Yi Jing Mastery – Module Two
Plum Blossom Numerology

Shao Yong, widely regarded as one of the greatest scholars of the Sung Dynasty, developed Mei Hua Yi Shu (Plum Blossom Numerology) as a more advanced means for divination purpose using the Yi Jing. In Plum Blossom Numerology, the results of a hexagram are interpreted by referring to the Gua meanings, where the interaction and relationship between the five elements, stems, branches and time are equally taken into consideration. This divination method, properly applied, allows us to make proper decisions whenever we find ourselves in a predicament.

Ze Ri Mastery Series™
LIVE COURSES (MODULES ONE AND TWO)

Ze Ri Mastery Series Module 1
Personal and Feng Shui Date Selection

The Mastery Academy's Date Selection Mastery Series Module 1 is specifically structured to provide novice students with an exciting introduction to the Art of Date Selection. Learn the rudiments and tenets of this intriguing metaphysical science. What makes a good date, and what makes a bad date? What dates are suitable for which activities, and what dates simply aren't? And of course, the mother of all questions: WHY aren't all dates created equal. All in only one Module – Module 1!

Ze Ri Mastery Series Module 2
Xuan Kong Da Gua Date Selection

In Module 2, discover advanced Date Selection techniques that will take your knowledge of this Art to a level equivalent to that of a professional's! This is the Module where Date Selection infuses knowledge of the ancient metaphysical science of Feng Shui and BaZi (Chinese Astrology, or Four Pillars of Destiny). Feng Shui, as a means of maximizing Human Luck (i.e. our luck on Earth), is often quoted as the cure to BaZi, which allows us to decipher our Heaven (i.e. inherent) Luck. And one of the most potent ways of making the most of what life has to offer us is to understand our Destiny, know how we can use the natural energies of our environment for our environments and MOST importantly, WHEN we should use these energies and for WHAT endeavors!

You will learn specific methods on how to select suitable dates, tailored to specific activities and events. More importantly, you will also be taught how to suit dates to a person's BaZi (Chinese Astrology, or Four Pillars of Destiny), in order to maximize his or her strengths, and allow this person to surmount any challenges that lie in wait. Add in the factor of `place', and you would have satisfied the notion of `doing the right thing, at the right time and in the right place'! A basic knowledge of BaZi and Feng Shui will come in handy in this Module, although these are not pre-requisites to successfully undergo Module 2.

Feng Shui for Life

Feng Shui for life is a 5-day course designed for the Feng Shui beginner to learn how to apply practical Feng Shui in day-to-day living. It is a culmination of powerful tools and techniques that allows you to gain quick proficiency in Classical Feng Shui. Discover quick tips on analysing your own BaZi, how to apply Feng Shui solutions for your own home, how to select auspicious dates for important activities, as well as simple and useful Face Reading techniques and practical Water Formulas. This is a complete beginner's course that is suitable for anyone with an interest in applying practical, real-world Feng Shui for life! Enhance every aspect of your life – your health, wealth, and relationships – using these easy-to-apply Classical Feng Shui methods.